PUTTING UNIVERSAL HUMAN RIGHTS TO WORK

PUTTING UNIVERSAL HUMAN RIGHTS TO WORK

Policy Actions in the Struggle For Social Justice

by

Archibald Stuart, Ph.D.

Gordian Knot Books

An Imprint of Richard Altschuler & Associates, Inc.

New York

Distributed by University Press of New England
Hanover and London

Putting Universal Human Rights to Work: Policy Actions in the Struggle for Social Justice. Copyright © 2012 by Archibald Stuart. For information write to the publisher, Richard Altschuler & Associates, Inc., at 100 West 57th Street, New York, NY 10019, call (212) 397-7233, or send an email to Richard.Altschuler@gmail.com.

Library of Congress Control Number: 2012906376
CIP data for this book are available from the Library of Congress

ISBN-13: 978-1-884092-83-1
ISBN-10: 1-884092-83-7

Gordian Knot Books is an imprint of
Richard Altschuler & Associates, Inc.

Cover Design: Josh Garfield

Printed in the United States of America

Distributed by University Press of New England
1 Court Street
Lebanon, New Hampshire 03766

TABLE OF CONTENTS

Preface

Putting Universal Human Rights to Work is written as a summary of what a large portion of my life has been about. I have run the race that has been set before me that probably has not been that dynamic, and is better described as treading the path that has been presented to me. It all started by growing up in the '30s amid the Great Depression, which found almost a quarter of the labor force unemployed. I vividly remember seeing hundreds of unemployed poor who were put to work in the federal Works Progress Administration program. I refer to this in the book and want to reestablish it as a way to serve the able-bodied unemployed poor.

Growing up I attended a public school in an affluent suburb where "home boys" were a part of the class. The boys had been removed from their parents, not for abuse or neglect, but were in a boys institution solely because of unemployment and poverty. I also saw the effect of the passage of the Social Security Act of 1935 that established the federal-state Aid to Dependent Children public assistance program, which provided aid on a case basis to all eligible families with children in their own homes. That program sent the "home boys" at my school back to their families. Our class picture shows a much smaller seventh grade class without them. Little did I know then how much this would stick in my memory, when the Aid to Dependent Children program was ended by the passage of the "welfare reform act" that removed many children, especially African Americans, off the welfare rolls. This resulted in a vast number of children who were deprived of basic human rights, housing and other essentials, which in the book I call one of the most infamous oppressive acts ever passed by the national Congress. I had always been interested in the social sciences and partly due to exposure to the social gospel through church activities, and acquiring a stepfather who was in social work, I became interested in the cause of social justice.

The 1940s saw me fighting in Germany, in World War II, in a field artillery unit. Serving in Europe made me more aware of the class struggle, as Europe is more class conscious than America. Following the war I was off to Harvard College, where I majored in economics and wrote a dissertation on labor relations dealing with collective bargaining. The Harvard economics department was one of the foundations of the New Deal of the Roosevelt years, based primarily on the macro-economic theories of John Maynard Keynes. He focused on the political economy and economic planning for full employment that turned me into a lifelong New Deal liberal, dedicated to a progressive ideology, which is the foundation for this book. The book deals with the struggle for social justice comprehensively, and introduces concepts of macroeconomics that are the basis for most of the policies discussed here. They need to be understood especially when dealing with the differences between equality of opportunity and equality of condition that arose in the 1960s, as part of the poverty program discussed at length in this book.

After Harvard I earned a masters degree in social work from the University of Chicago School of Social Service Administration. Social work practice in those days consisted mostly of individual casework, dealing with the social-emotional functioning of individual cases that made much use of psychoanalytic theory. To this I had no special talents, as social work did not draw on my macro-economic background. After a number of years I got the opportunity to teach social welfare policy, planning and community organization at the University of Connecticut School of Social Work, where I taught for thirty years. During that time I was able to study social welfare policy and planning at the Heller School of Social Welfare at Brandeis University, where I received a doctorate in 1971.

The decision to write this book came after my retirement, when I was stricken with a near-fatal infection that cost me the vision in one eye and left me with the ability to read only by use of a magnifying machine. I discovered that I could write using a magnifier on the computer.

I want to especially thank attorney Phillip Tegeler of the Poverty & Race Research Action Council (PRRAC), Maggie Adair, formerly of Connecticut Association for Human Services, Jane McNichol of the Legal Assistance Research Center of Connecticut, attorney David Furie of the Hartford office of the U.S. Department of Housing and Urban Development, Jeff Freiser of Connecticut Housing Coalition, and Walter Glomb of the University of Connecticut Center for Excellence in Developmental Disabilities Education. The Connecticut Association for Human Services assisted with the editing, and I want to especially thank the executive director, Jim Horan, and staff member Marci Neufer for helping with the notes and editing.

What I have tried to do in the book is present policy action in the struggle for social justice. I have defined social justice as the increase of socio-economic equality, the provision of human rights—mainly the United Nation's Universal Declaration of Human Rights—and the provision of social security. The objective is stated as the provision of human rights, rather than the reduction of those in poverty, which tends to lead to blaming the victim and use of token food programs that mostly serve to enhance the esteem of the givers rather than providing anything substantive.

The book's focus is on the *struggle* for social justice, as there is not much indication of making recent progress. This is because of the growing power of conservative forces, the decline in the number of persons employed in manufacturing, and a dramatic decline in union membership.

I have tried to address needed policy action comprehensively, dealing first with differences in ideologies that, for analytical purposes, I have termed laissez-fare conservatives and social liberals.

That is over simplified but seems to catch the main ideological differences. I also emphasized the opposing forces individuals and groups face, one being the need for social dominance and the other being the need for sharing togetherness and equality. I tried to comprehensively review all policies that have a major effect on social justice, including employment, wages, labor relations, social welfare, education and civil rights, so that the entire possibility for action is covered and policies are placed in proper perspective.

I felt the need for more information about how to continue to reduce the gap between the earnings of whites and African Americans, which has stalled in the last thirty or so years, and seems to indicate that most whites, with their need for social dominance, feel more threatened as the gap closes. I tried to be especially comprehensive in regard to social welfare, by including both occupational welfare, which deals with employer programs, and fiscal welfare, which deals with tax relief in the form of deductions, tax credits and tax disregards.

In social welfare, I looked at the use of universal benefits, social insurance, and means-tested programs applied to both cash and special benefit programs for nutrition, health care, housing and the handicapped. In dealing with education and civil rights, I tried to point out that there were forces working both for and against quality and social justice. In looking at needed policy actions I focused on existing policies and, therefore, on what are likely feasible developments. I tried to make the analysis of needed policy actions complete by ending the book with a discussion of the use of political action strategies and organizing for political action.

I like to feel that I am not personally involved in the struggle for social justice due to some special need. My background was clearly upper-middle class and I am an Anglo-Saxon male. I therefore would like to think that my involvement is strictly ideo-logical, and that in writing the book I am being fair to all interests, even though I realize this is never entirely possible. Hence I deliberately refrained from any personal references and do not use "I" or "we."

I offer this book as my "swan song" to leave behind, and hope that many academic programs will find it useful and inspiring. I hope that it will prove useful in courses dealing with human rights and provide ideas for policy actions. Also, I hope that it will be useful in courses dealing with public policy, social policy, social welfare policy and human services. Further, I would like to think that it would be useful in professional graduate schools of social work, law, medicine, nursing and seminaries to address concerns they have for social justice policies.

Finally, I would like to dedicate this book to the memory of my stepfather, Bleecker Marquette, who was such an inspiration for justice in the areas of health and housing. This work is also dedicated to the memory of my former colleague, Professor Benjamin Beyrer, who was such an inspiration in social welfare policy, and lastly to all those who feel challenged to engage in policy actions in the struggle for social justice.

Chapter 1

Introduction

One of the most basic social processes is the struggle for social justice. The struggle is a struggle for social equality, especially in civil and human rights, social power, distribution of wealth and income, and for socio-economic security. It is based on the belief that all humans are created with equal needs and have dignity and worth. The struggle can be understood as a counterforce to the social-psychological need of individuals and collectivities for social dominance in a competitive struggle for esteem, security, income, wealth, and power (Sidanius & Pratto, 1999). In contrast, social justice involves equality, togetherness, cooperation, sharing and mutuality.

All societies need a hierarchal system that gives higher status and authority to individuals, groups and collectivities. At the same time, societies need a community system based on equal rights and responsibilities with an emphasis on commonality and belongingness. One of the basic social processes is seen as a struggle between these two forces. Some societies lend themselves to more centralization of power and authority. An example is in a society with less need for skilled labor where a centralized authority tells workers what to do, and oversees their doing it in a master-servant relationship that fosters serfdom and slavery. More industrial societies that require a wide variety of skills rely more on partnership and cooperation.

Ideally a society based on partnership and cooperation would act like a symphony orchestra where specialists in playing various musical instruments come together to perform—a common task in a partnership that requires each to be treated with some degree of equality. In capitalist societies the struggle for social justice mainly takes the form of the struggle for the economic and social rights of employees, which is often referred to as the "class struggle." The functioning of the competitive market economy is based on winners and losers and results in a concentration of wealth and economic power by the owners and managers of capital. In many societies, the struggle for social justice is further complicated by the social dominance needs of racial, ethnic, and religious groups, as well as other social organizations. The task becomes more difficult to the extent that it challenges the existing socio-economic order.

The struggle for social justice also involves the dominance of various values and ideologies. Advocates of social-economic dominance emphasize such values as social Darwinism based on the natural process of survival of the fittest, which calls for those proven fit to be rewarded. There is also emphasis on the justice of the market, which rewards efficiency and productivity and allocates the distribution of goods and services where they are most needed and valued.

Social justice draws on religious values and social ethics. Social justice is often regarded as the corporate expression of the love for others. In Christianity these values are often seen as included in what is called the social gospel or in Latin America as liberation theology (Wallis, 2005). Social justice draws heavily on the ethic of reciprocity expressed in the Golden Rule: "Do unto others as you would have them do unto you." Fairness is regarded as reciprocity between the legitimate social needs and rights of persons and social obligations of others to provide and protect them. Similarly, legal justice is seen as basically dealing with the balance between rights and obligations that involves compensation and reciprocity in providing rewards and punishments. Democratic values involve not only the right to vote and civil rights, but also human rights. An expression of the ethos of social justice as based on human rights in a democratic society are these memorable lines from the Declaration of Independence: "We hold these truths to be self-evident, that all men are created equal, that they are endowed by their Creator with certain inalienable Rights, that among these are Life, Liberty, and the pursuit of Happiness. That to secure these Rights, Governments are instituted among Men, deriving their just powers from the consent of the governed."

The values of social justice are also well expressed in the battle cry of the French Revolution: "*Liberté, Égalité, Fraternité.*" *Liberté* is the freedom and opportunity to develop and utilize one's full capacities for the fulfillment of self and others; *Égalité* is the right to socio-economic equality; and *Fraternité* involves together-ness, sharing, and mutuality.

Analysis of the Struggle

One way to frustrate social reform efforts is to define objectives in global, abstract terms, such as doing what is most loving, peaceful, and against violence, and eliminating poverty. One nods his head in agreement, but is lost as to what action to take and often re-sponds in token ways, such as operating a soup kitchen to eliminate poverty. Social justice can be a vague and abstract objective unless concepts and steps for action are defined in detail. This piece is an attempt to do so. What follows is an effort to define the objectives of social justice, provide a basic analysis of what policy actions are needed, and look at how well existing policies are working. Included in the discussion is an estimation of what would be the most effective and politically feasible develop-ments toward social justice. Because much of the struggle to bring about policy action is viewed as a clash between liberal and conservative forces, this book will look at each of their ideologies and political and social strengths. Indicated policy actions will be looked at comprehensively, to give proper perspective and identify where action is most needed.

For analytical purposes, the struggle will be broken down into two main social systems that are involved. One is the employment, wages and labor relations system, which involves public and private policies and programs dealing with jobs, unemployment, job security, wages, hours, working conditions and labor relations. The second main system is the social welfare system, which provides benefits for health, housing, nutrition, economic security and social services. It generally provides these benefits in non-market exchanges that are not paid as an exchange for services rendered.

The social welfare system will be broken down into three components: 1) the occupational welfare system, which consists of employee benefits paid to workers in addition to wages; 2) fiscal welfare, which consists of benefits paid in the form of tax deductions, credits, exemptions, and rates paid; and 3) social welfare benefits paid to eligible persons by public and private social welfare agencies. These benefits are supported mainly by public funds and paid either in cash or by providing items such as housing and medical care insurance to eligible individuals.

A third system could be termed the civil rights system, which is mainly concerned with the equal treatment of individuals before the law; with freedom from discrimination due to factors such as age, sex, race, handicaps, and ethnicity; and with equality of opportunity for education, employment and other social statuses.

Other important systems are the education system, which provides persons with needed knowledge and skills; and the infrastructure system, which provides services such as transportation, public utilities, and financial services. In these systems, social justice is regarded as not just meaning that all receive equal treatment, but that people are treated according to their needs, such as more help with the learning needs of the disadvantaged and public transportation for those who cannot afford to own a car. An analysis will be made of the social and political forces affecting each system and, in this light, to suggest what feasible policy developments and social action strategies are called for. The purpose of this comprehensive analysis is to identify trends in the struggle for social justice in each system so that the struggle can be seen in proper perspective, e.g., that the civil rights system has not lessened the gap between the earnings of African Americans and those of whites in the last thirty or so years. This comprehensive analysis deals with the interaction of different systems. For example, conservatives have blamed unemployment and low-wage jobs on the lack of education of the victims. The facts indicate, however, that this is a matter of the functioning of the economic system, and that greater educational attainment has little effect on the rate of unemployment or the number of low-wage jobs.

This book, in essence, will explore political factors that affect policy developments and suggest means of building political support for indicated actions. The analysis will be applied to the struggle in the United States, but the same analytical concepts should be applied to efforts to promote social justice in other nations through foreign trade, foreign aid and other foreign policies.

The Struggle Past to Present

The celebration in 2007 of the two-hundredth anniversary of the abolition of the slave trade in the British Empire serves as a reminder that slavery is one of the places in recent times where the struggle for social justice began. The work of William Wilberforce in getting the abolition through Parliament is an example of using governmental processes to change the existing socio-economic order, and of countering the power of those who benefited by it. This was easier to do in Britain, where slavery was less entrenched, than in the U.S.

Following the abolition movement, significant efforts for social justice in the U.S. included the effort to end child labor, which was strongly opposed as unjust interference in the labor market system; the passage of the federal income tax amendment in 1913, which made income transfers more possible as part of the welfare state, based on the concept of "from each according to his ability, to each according to his need"; and the passage of the women's suffrage amendment in 1919, which led to giving more civil and economic power to women.

The most significant thrust for social justice occurred largely as a result of the breakdown of the market economy during the Great Depression. Most significant was the passage of the federal Social Security Act in 1935, which was regarded as the beginning of the welfare state with its provisions for economic security as an entitlement (Trattner,1999).The act established the social insurance systems of Old Age, Survivors, and Disability Insurance, and the federal-state system of unemployment compensation. It also established a federal-state system of public assistance for children, the blind, and disabled, which was provided as a right for all eligible persons. Important in the Depression period was the growth of labor movements organized by industries and not just by trades. Labor became a real force for social justice, not only in dealing with wages and working conditions but, also, as the principal advocate for public policies for social justice. This growth was aided by the passage of the National Labor Relations Act in 1935, which provided protection for labor unions to organize and engage in collective bargaining, and the Fair Labor Standards Act in 1938, which dealt with wages and hours and working conditions.

The Depression period led to the development of the concept of the political economy, which refers to the idea that governmental fiscal and monetary policies could be used to affect the functioning of the economy, especially in dealing with unemployment and economic growth. A special feature of this was the use of the fiscal policy of deficit spending to stimulate economic growth and full employment. This involved expenditures for public works such as highways, conservation and public housing. Another feature of the political economy was the use of agricultural price supports to assure farmers a decent income from their products.

The concept of the political economy was further fostered during World War II with the creation of price controls. In the post-war era, social justice objectives of equality in economic status and opportunity were fostered by the provision of various veterans' benefits, such as the G.I. bills for higher education and low-interest home loans. In the immediate post-war period, the pent-up demand for goods and services that were not available during the war resulted in great economic growth and investment in modern production, which increased the productivity of labor.

Through the efforts of the industrial unions (such as the auto and steel workers' unions), increased productivity led to increased wages and employee benefits, so that many workers could enjoy middle class status. It was more possible for disadvantaged minorities to share in the growth that gave them more power. This led in the 1960s to the Civil Rights Movement, which resulted in the federal Civil Rights Act, which addressed discrimination in employment, housing, and education. Equally significant was the passage of the Voting Rights Act, which abolished racial discrimination in elections. The civil rights movement of the '60s led to the federal poverty program, with a special emphasis on education and training programs to provide equal opportunity for minorities and women. It also promoted community organizing for social action directed at local needs for education, social welfare services, housing, and economic development.

A significant development was the establishment of the federal Medicare program. It provided the elderly and disabled with federal healthcare insurance and established the federal-state Medicaid program, which provided hospital, nursing home, and longterm medical care for poor families with children, the disabled and the aged. Another development was the federal Supplementary Security program, which established a national minimum income benefit for needy blind, disabled and aged individuals whose critical needs were not met through Social Security benefits. The federal Food Stamp Program was established to provide better nutrition for needy persons. There were also new federal-state programs established for economic development and affordable housing.

By the mid-1970s, the long period of economic growth slowed, as did most progress toward social justice. One event that signaled the end of progress was the failure to pass the Family Assistance Plan proposed by the Nixon administration. The plan was conceived as a way to establish a negative income tax that would provide a national benefit for all families with incomes under $2,400. This figure proved to be too high for low-income states, which would have upset their existing socio-economic order; and it would have been below the welfare grant level in high-income states. This failure was followed by a period of conservatism that has largely continued since. The decline in economic growth resulted in unemployment and a decline of high-income manufacturing jobs, which were further reduced by outsourcing many manufacturing jobs. These longterm trends, in turn, led to a marked decline in union membership.

The economic decline threatened low-income whites who were afraid of being displaced by African Americans who sought higher education as a means of competing for scarce, good jobs. The result was a backlash against the Civil Rights Movement that led many whites to shift to the conservative Republican party. The loss of the economic growth dividend to fund social welfare programs meant that further progress would depend on tax increases opposed by most conservatives. The growing conservatism culminated in the election of President Reagan in 1980, effectively ending progress toward social justice. One of the first actions taken by the Reagan administration was to fire the air-traffic controllers who were on strike, which further weakened the labor movement. Most social welfare programs, including subsidies for affordable housing, were severely cut. This was clearly a form of racial oppression aimed at African Americans, who had become disproportionately represented in welfare programs (Phillips, 1990).

8

All of this contributed to a growing inequality in real family income in the postwar period to 1979, and from there to 2003 (see Table 1.1 below). The virtually equal increase in all the quintiles up to 1979 was undone in the period since, when the income of the lowest quintile dropped by 2 percent whereas the income of the top quintile increased by 51 percent.

Table 1.1
Percentage Increase In National Income
By Quintiles, 1979-2003

Quintile	Percent increase 1947 to 1979		Percent increase 1979 to 2003	
Lowest 20%	Up to $7,000	116%	Up to $24,100	-2%
Second 20%	$7,000-$13,000	100%	$24,100-$42,100	8%
Third 20%	$13,000-$20,000	111%	$42,100-$65,000	15%
Fourth 20%	$20,000-$29,100	114%	$65,000-$98,000	26%
Highest 20%	$29,100 and Up	99%	$98,000 and Up	51%

Source: Collins & Yeskel, 2005

The result has been that inequality in income distribution has increased when measured by the percent of total income distribution by quintiles (see Table 1.2 on the next page). Noteworthy is the increase in the percentages going to the top fifth and the top 5 percent: In 2005 the top 5 percent received 21.7 percent of the national income, greater than the bottom two quintiles combined at 13.6 percent. To reverse this trend represents a basic challenge in the struggle for social justice. Those with incomes below 125 percent of the poverty line (a better measure of real poverty) was reduced from 30.4 percent in 1960 to 18.2 percent in 1980, but only slightly since then, to 16.8 percent in 2005. These trends will be explored in detail concerning policy action in the following chapters.

Table 1.2

Percentage Distribution of Household Income by Quintiles, 1970-2009

Year	Lowest Quintile	Second Quintile	Third Quintile	Fourth Quintile	Highest Quintile
1970	4.1	10.8	17.4	24.5	43.5
1980	4.2	10.2	16.8	24.7	44.1
1990	3.8	9.6	15.9	24.0	46.6
2000	3.6	8.9	14.9	23.2	49.4
2009	3.4	8.6	14.6	23.2	50.3

Source: DeNavas-Walt, Proctor, & Smith, 2010

Chapter 2

The Struggle of Laissez -Faire Conservatism Versus Social Liberalism

The struggle for social justice can best be understood as a conflict between justice of the private market system, with its focus on competition and just prices for labor, goods and services, and the concept of social justice, with its focus on equality, cooperation and mutuality (Kuttner, 1992; 1999). The concept of justice in the private market system leads to an ethos that is often termed rightist, capitalist, conservative or free market. Its advocates prefer to use the term "free market," but note that persons often are not as free to shop for lower prices or for higher wages, due to the lack of competition, as its advocates would like one to believe. Critics cite many examples of where the so-called free market does not work and becomes a means for human oppression. One example is when a landlord charges rent that he knows a renter cannot afford, but the landlord is aware the market will not supply renters with cheaper affordable rent, even though housing is an essential need. Thus, for purposes of this discussion, it might best be termed "laissez-faire conservatism."

Laissez-faire conservatism expresses the theme that the uncontrolled private market should dominate the social and economic process and the notion that the best government is one that governs least. The concept is that the competitive marketplace exchange balances supply and demand that sets a true value on goods and services. This assures that resources, including labor, are allocated where they are most needed and hence most valued. The private market system also serves the ethos of consumer sovereignty: that consumers should be free to spend their funds for that which they value most. The marketplace is sometimes depicted as the "invisible hand" that guides this allocation of resources to where they are most needed and most valued.

One of the often cited merits of the competitive market system is that it promotes efficiency as it seeks the most cost effective use of resources and labor. Thus there is criticism of products and services provided by governments, where there is no competition, as promoting waste and poor quality. Laissez-faire conservatives would prefer that governments contract out most production and services to private enterprises that can compete with each other in bidding for the contract. In regard to wages, the quest for efficiency is seen as an incentive to increase the productivity of labor through such devices as automation, so that the labor costs per unit of output are lowered. Hence, wages can be increased without increasing prices so that the standard of living can be raised.

There is always an effort for businesses to hold down labor costs and lower prices to increase the share of the market and enjoy the profits of scale. This has been well illustrated by the low labor costs, low prices, and high volume success of the discount department store Walmart. Thus the main objective is to pay only subsistence wages for workers, particularly in labor intensive employments such as farming and soft goods production that require a large number of workers to produce low priced goods. Much of human oppression has been a consequence of the need for low cost farm labor that led to serfdom, slavery, and bondage. To get a large supply of low cost labor, employers have often imported workers from foreign countries where they were accustomed to a low standard of living, and also lacked language and other skills that would enable them to compete for better jobs. This need for low cost labor is now being carried out in the employment of illegal immigrants, who are often employed in a black market at below minimum wages and without other labor protections and few civil rights.

Basically employers like a pool of unemployed workers that are available to fill jobs at low costs. In the height of the boom in the 1990s Alan Greenspan, then the head of the Federal Reserve, expressed concern that a tight labor market with low unemployment would raise wages and spur inflation. Thus many employers were not terribly concerned about the amount of unemployment. Generally employers have resisted any interference in the labor market. Throughout much of the nineteenth century they even fought efforts to prevent the hiring of child labor at very low wages. They have generally opposed labor organizing and collective bargaining and fought any legislation to protect the rights of labor. Wages paid to the lowest paid laborers have generally established a baseline, with higher wages being offered for what is needed to attract workers with the required skills. Most employers have sought to pay wages, especially in labor intensive employment, that is the minimum required for basic necessities; and they have resisted paying what is regarded as a living wage. Laissez-faire conservatives have also resisted the payment of social welfare benefits, especially to able-bodied workers, that are not earned in the labor market, as this interferes with the functioning of the labor market, which pays wages in exchange for labor. This issue will be discussed in further detail when looking at the functioning of the social welfare system.

All of this points to a survival of the fittest ethos in the competition for jobs, which draws on the social-psychological need for social dominance. That leads to the ethic of individualism in which each person is seen as master of his own fate, responsible for his own self-sufficiency and entitled to the rewards of his labor. Employment and higher wages are incentives to acquire greater skills and to work harder. In this competitive system there are both winners and losers, so there are both rich and poor, and the goal is not to provide greater equality of income. Extremists would advocate that the winners deserve to win big and the losers to lose big, as this is needed for incentives to make them try harder. In order to increase incentives, most laissez-faire conservatives seek equality of opportunity, to give each person an equal chance to acquire the skills needed to compete for various employments. Equality of opportunity is seen as best provided by making available equal educational opportunities for all, often with special help for the disadvantaged. Hence, poverty and unemployment are regarded as the fault of the individual for lacking the attributes to succeed in the competitive labor market. The ethos of individualism resists taxes, especially income taxes that are progressive and tax higher incomes at higher rates, and hence deprive persons of the fruits of their labor and weaken incentives to earn more.

The so-called "Protestant ethic"—with its emphasis on individual salvation and the personal ethic of abstinence and hard work—is suited to justifying this inequality, as the winners are regarded as being more moral, hard working, and self-sufficient persons. The poor are usually labeled as immoral and undeserving of help. This was beautifully satirized by George Bernard Shaw in the play "Pygmalion" and was included in the musical "My Fair Lady" when Liza's father, Alfred Doolittle, who is a dustman, says he was one of the undeserving poor but had a right to basic sustenance; and that he couldn't afford middle class morals but had a right to live his own lifestyle (Shaw, 1951). Clearly he saw his fate as the position he was forced to occupy in the competitive social order, and that if he did not occupy it someone else would. In this ethos the labor market system is taken as a given method of just economic allocation.

The conservative laissez-faire ethos places emphasis on maintaining the current system, with an emphasis on social control and maintenance of the prevailing value system. This leads to a focus on the rights of individuals to protection from harm by others and deviancy control rather than on economic rights, such as to a decent standard of living. There are many examples of this, including an emphasis on protecting children from abuse and neglect rather than providing their families with the right to decent affordable housing, which has been shown is a main factor in fostering child development. Another example is a focus on the alcohol and drug problems of the poor rather than the right to a job at a living wage.

Those who embrace laissez-faire conservatism are mostly from the upper socio-economic class. There are obvious extremes within what is called laissez-faire conservatism. At one end are the libertarians, who would have almost all economic activity in the private market, including schools and public services such as roads and parks. Those lacking income for basic necessities such medical care and schooling would have to depend on private charity from churches and civic associations. At the other extreme are those who accept that many services cannot be supplied by the private market and private charity, and that there is a need for public services and public funding for schools, social welfare and health care. Also they would see the private market as increasingly needing governmental regulation if it is to function with fairness and protect the rights of individuals and organizations. Yet the laissez-faire conservatives have shown themselves to be unified in preferring that the private market be the predominant economic system; and they view the distribution of income by the private labor market as just and high incomes as needed for investment and growth. Hence, laissez-faire conservatives are generally opposed to efforts that address the class struggle, especially as it involves labor unions and income and property taxes.

The Ideology of Social Liberalism

The basic ethos of the struggle for social justice relies heavily on what can be termed social liberalism, which is concerned with the social order and social conditions. It is based on a belief in the dignity and worth of each individual, with each individual having both civil rights, such as the right to vote and equality before the law, and human rights, such as the right to safety, protection, security and to a decent standard of living. This concern includes provision for what is needed for one's personal development, including economic and social security, education, and opportunities for personal growth.

Those advocating for social justice embrace the ideals expressed in the United Nations *Universal Declaration of Human Rights*. It includes civil rights, such as equality before the law, the rights to privacy and freedom of speech and religion, and the right to participate in government and free elections. It also includes economic rights, such as the right to desirable work, the right to join trade unions, and the right to a "standard of living adequate to the health and well-being of himself and of his family" (United Nations, 1948, Article 25).

The basic ethos of social liberalism is one of social equality, togetherness, cooperation, mutual support and sharing. As an example, one remembers being in Gatwick airport in England about to fly back to the U.S. and hearing the airplane pilot announce that the plane could not take off until the toilets were unplugged. This is not to suggest that the pilot and the toilet cleaner be paid the same, but there needs to be some recognition that each is a necessary member of the employee team, who is entitled to some semblance of equality. Ideally this would mean that there would be no more inequality of income than that needed for the division of labor, and equal employment rights such as job security and employee benefits.

Social justice is concerned with social conditions, especially the distribution of income, wealth, and social power. The focus is not on each separate individual but the wellbeing of collectivities in a community: families and children, the aged, the handicapped, the unemployed, skilled and unskilled labor and minority groups. As in public health, social justice is concerned with the incidence (the number of new cases) and the prevalence (the number of ongoing cases) of human conditions such as poverty and unemployment. As such it deals with facts, statistics and survey research, not with anecdotes of individual situations regarding successes and failures.

Rather than seeing individuals as masters of their own fate—as a consequence of how they succeed in a competitive market—social liberalism sees individuals as the beneficiaries or victims of social conditions mostly beyond their individual control. Hence in order to further social justice, it seeks to deal with social conditions, such as unemployment and unequal distribution of income, by calling for public policy interventions in socio-economic systems that the market economy either cannot correct by itself or sees as justified for the optimum functioning of the economy.

The Economies of Laissez-faire and Social Justice

As was noted, the ideology of laissez-faire conservatism is based on the concept of the invisible hand of the market, which sets the optimum price that matches supply and demand. However, it is agreed it only works in a perfect market in which there are many buyers and sellers so that the action of any one cannot affect the price. Liberal economists such as John Kenneth Galbraith have pointed out that the attributes of perfect competition are found in such places as commodity markets and the stock markets, where there are a large number of buyers and sellers, but does not fit most modern industrial markets, which are dominated by a few large corporations where there are few buyers and sellers. The latter constitute monopolies and oligopolies that can determine among themselves what prices they will charge buyers or pay sellers (Galbraith, 1993). Thus the optimum price and distribution of goods and services is not achieved. Buyers face prices they cannot afford and suppliers struggle with low prices for goods and services that do not adequately cover costs. For example, in a labor market where there are few large employers, they can generally agree among themselves what wages to pay for various types of labor; and except for highly skilled professional positions, individual workers have virtually no bargaining power in seeking higher wages. That has led to the development of labor unions that can

17

bargain collectively for wages and benefits based on the threat of strikes or job actions.

Economists such as Galbraith have pointed out that the lack of real competition in setting prices has been replaced by corporations marketing their products: instead of responding to demand through price competition, they create demand by marketing activities for goods and services that they sell at a given price. Galbraith (1993) argued that this lack of price competition calls for public policies that use various countervailing powers to force bargaining. One example is labor legislation that allows employees to organize trade unions and requires employers to engage in collective bargaining. Also, large buyers can countervail the power of a few large sellers. An example is car rental companies that bargain with auto companies when they buy a large number of cars. This leads to public policies that facilitate the organization of buyer co-ops and consortia that can bargain for lower prices. The use of a few large buyers is being advocated for in healthcare reform, by encouraging the organization of large pools of health insurance buyers to come together to bargain with insurance companies for lower rates.

The lack of price competition has led social liberals to advocate for government price controls, especially for essential goods and services where low prices are needed. Price control has traditionally been used for public utilities where there can be only one supplier. Recently, laissez-faire conservatives have sought to deregulate controlled prices to create competitive markets. Many analysts are of the opinion that where this has been done the results have been mixed. One effort has been to deregulate utilities by providing competition for the generation of electric power. Many analysts feel this has not reduced prices for individual consumers but mainly for large consumers such as businesses. Many also are of the opinion that the deregulation of airfare has led to a decline in the quality of service and created chaos in air fares, with airlines choosing among themselves where and when they will compete. Airfare often has little relationship with the distance of the flight.

Many social liberals point to places where price controls are clearly needed. One instance is to deal with the problem of consumers who are overburdened with debt, by setting controls on credit card interest charges where the banks have shown little competition among themselves. Also there is considerable use of government subsidies and tax reductions to make needed goods and services such as food, housing, and medical care more affordable. In many instances price controls need to accompany public subsidies so that they will not just be passed on in higher prices. This needs to be considered in connection with subsidies of medical insurance premiums so it will not lead to higher rates.

Finally it needs to be noted that sellers of the same product do not just compete among themselves, but also with the sellers of other goods and services for discretionary spending, and thus need to sell their products for prices that are affordable. This has led to mass production of many items that are sold at low, affordable prices. Here one thinks of Henry Ford who started the mass production of affordable autos, which was followed by the production of many other items, including appliances, computers and communication devices, that put such things as televisions and air conditioners in virtually every home. This has resulted in both huge increases in worker productivity, due to high volume production, and higher wages, making more items affordable and raising the standard of living—a phenomenon recognized as the great American success. However, with the development of a world economy, much of this production has gone overseas to take advantage of lower wages. This has helped to raise the standard of living in much of the world, but threatens to harm the American economy, unless there is protection from losing too many high- wage jobs.

Social liberalism sees laissez-faire conservatism as failing to provide for equality in human conditions and, in fact, leading to a higher concentration of income, wealth and social power. When the owners of capital reinvest their returns in more capital it grows, in geometrical proportion. Thus, for example, an annual rate of return of about 7 percent, when reinvested, doubles the investment every 10 years. The result is that the more capital one has the more it grows, leading to an increased concentration of wealth. It has not been generally noticed until very recently how concentrated and ever-increasing this is. In 1976 the top 1 percent of households owned 22 percent of all wealth, including savings, equities and real property. By 2001 the portion of wealth held by the top 1 percent had increased to an overwhelming 38 percent (Wolff, 2002).

Social liberalism sees most social conditions as a consequence of processes in the socio-economic order not due to the attributes and behavior of individuals. This was illustrated during the Great Depression when unemployment was as much as 20 percent; and following WWII pent-up demand led to increased spending and investment opportunities that dropped unemployment to below 5 percent. The increasing inequality of income cannot be explained by any change in individual attributes such as motivation, level of education, or work habits. That calls for attention to factors that affect the functioning of the economy as a whole. The private market system focuses on each individual transaction in the market and not on the aggregate impact of numerous transactions. Human service workers, with their focus on individual cases, often assume that every time an individual gets a job it adds to the volume of employment rather than having replaced someone else in the competition for scarce jobs. This leads to confusing broad social problems such as the level of unemployment with problems of individuals and, consequently, to "blaming the victim" as being untrained or unmotivated. Economist, Leon Keyserling used the analogy of looking at who drowned in the sinking of the Titanic to explain the blame that occurs during challenging economic times. When the Titanic sank, more women and children were saved, while many men drowned. Keyserling suggested, based on statistics, that it appeared men died because of their characteristics, but the fact is that more men died because there weren't enough life boats.

In economic analysis, there is the dichotomy of "micro" versus "macro." Micro-economic analysis deals with individual market transactions that mainly serve to establish prices. Conversely, macro-economic analysis deals with the aggregate consequences of micro-economic transactions on the functioning of the economy as a whole, on aggregate income and on the aggregate demand for goods and services (Baumol & Blinder, 1986). It deals with the circular flow of economic activity from earned income to how it is spent in the purchasing of goods and services and investments that, in turn, produce earned income. The Great Depression was a consequence of a downward spiral in which less aggregate demand resulted in fewer sales that, in turn, led to less production and, hence, to more unemployment, which further reduced aggregate income. Conversely, the post-war years, with the pent-up demand created in the war years, produced an upward spiral in which increased aggregate demand led to an increase in income and employment.

It became clear that the laissez-faire market economy does not have within itself a major means for adjusting to reduced aggregate demand and unemployment. The classical argument of laissez-faire economics is that employment could be increased if workers were willing to work for lower wages, making it economical to hire workers in place of machines or to do some tasks made affordable by reduced labor costs. This was refuted with the development of macro-economic theory by Keynes (2006) and others, which established that the level of employment is a consequence of the aggregate demand for goods and services; and that, in fact, reducing personal income would reduce demand and increase unemployment.

A real test of this is to ask the following question: Could the nation achieve full employment by cutting wages in half? A micro-economic analysis calculation, with a focus on individual transactions, would conclude that this would be so, because employers could employ more workers. Conversely, a macro-economic analysis, with its emphasis on the circular flow, would conclude that the reverse would happen. If income were cut in half, this would result in a disastrous decline in the aggregate demand for goods and services, thus causing high unemployment. Micro-economic analysis has no real solution for aggregate national unemployment, whereas a macro-economic analysis suggests solutions. One example is increasing the demand for goods and services by implementing government fiscal policies such as deficit spending and income tax cuts for consumers. Policies for social justice that include higher wages, equality in the distribution of income, and social welfare expenditures that increase income are a major factor for increasing demand and produce an expansion of the production of goods and services.

The main effort that laissez-faire conservatives make to deal with aggregate effects of income is to advocate the idea of trickle-down economics, based on the assumption that as the rich get richer they will have more income to invest, leading to economic expansion that increases employment and growth of personal incomes. They see trickledown economics furthered by income tax cuts for the wealthy, which increase the amount of income available for investment and boost the incentive to invest due to fewer taxes on investment returns. Conversely, most of those using macro-economic analysis would say that amount of investment is not essentially based on the amount of income available to invest, but primarily on expected market returns based on the expected demand for more and better goods and services. Hence, when the economy was facing a downward spiral there would be less demand expected.

The Great Depression was the result of people having less to spend to support investments. An example is that airlines would be foolish to invest in more airplanes when there is not enough demand to fill existing seats. Trickledown economics is more concerned with economic expansion than equality. Statistics on distribution of income show there is not much evidence that recent tax cuts trickle down from the wealthy into more income for working people. Without increased investment opportunities, the wealthy may just use their increased income to acquire assets such as stocks and bonds and real estate rather than investments in economic growth, which leads only to a further concentration of wealth.

Social liberalism believes that economic expansion is best facilitated by trickle up policies that seek to increase demand by giving consumers more to spend. This is best achieved by increased productivity, so that labor costs per unit of output are decreased. Therefore higher wages can be paid without raising prices, producing an economic growth surplus that can be spent on increased demand for goods and services. This would best be facilitated by public policies that lower interest rates to fund investment in greater productivity; tax incentives to increase productivity; and an emphasis on professional and technical education to develop new and better products and increased productivity. Investment is also aided by lower interest rates that make it easier to fund investment opportunities. Public investment and controls in infrastructure, including roads, transportation, utilities, and financial services, can both increase productivity of these services and also make for conservation, economic stability, and more efficient use of energy and other resources.

The ideology of the political economy and macro-economic concepts rely on governmental policies and programs to promote employment, growth, and economic equality. This ideology is one of the main instruments for accomplishing the goals in the struggle for social justice. One use of the concept of political economy is economic planning for full employment, which seeks to increase employment in slack times through economic stimulus policies, such as tax cuts for consumers, and deficit spending that increases spending income. The concept of the political economy uses public policies for the redistribution of income to provide for human rights and greater equality, which is accomplished by increasing taxes on the wealthy to provide for social welfare programs. According to laissez-faire conservatives, increased taxes are a drag on the economy as taxpayers have less money to spend in the private market; but a macro-economic analysis indicates that payments for social welfare services, especially when financed by income taxes on the wealthy, are ways to increase demand and stimulate the economy. Benefits such as unemployment compensation help to keep up demand in the face of increased unemployment, and Social Security benefits give retirees income to spend, which keeps up demand that would be lost if a retiree had little income. What especially needs to be noted is that increased public payments for health and education services are used to meet the need for expanded employment and higher wages in these fields. Both fields require government funding for the investment needed to meet increased needs for facilities, equipment and professional skills. The implementation of the political economy that uses fiscal policies, public programs and public regulations as the foundation in the struggle for social justice will be dealt with in further detail in the sections that follow.

The struggle for social justice undeniably involves the struggle for equality in social power and empowering individuals to have control over their own affairs and wellbeing while respecting the rights and needs of others. Here an important ethos is the concept of "one man, one vote." It includes not only the right to vote but equalizes the ability to influence how people vote and conveys the idea that public policy decisions are not dominated by those with more wealth and status. This puts a focus on such things as campaign finance reform, control over lobbying activities, and control over advertising and public relations activities for political purposes. This might include such things as limiting the concentration of ownership of the media. Another goal is to broaden the base of power within both public and private organizations, such as giving employees powers in their own security and wellbeing through trade unions and other organizations that work for their interests. Yet another goal is to give consumers and investors some power to protect their own interests through participation in decision-making and organized activities that affect their welfare, plus some power to hold decision-makers accountable for their actions.

Equality of Opportunity Versus Equality of Condition

One focus of the civil rights movement of the 1960s was an emphasis on equality of opportunity to compete for scarce jobs. This became one of the main efforts of the anti-poverty program, which emphasized training and education for minorities and women, primarily to enable them to better compete for employment opportunities. What was largely ignored was any thought that this would displace others who would become the unemployed and low-paid poor. Its advocates seemed to imply that increased education and training would eliminate unemployment and low-paying jobs, whereas the facts were that this largely resulted in better educated unemployed and low-paid workers. That led to the seminal book by Ryan (1971) entitled *Blaming the Victim*, which became the rallying point for all those who wanted to emphasize full employment and better paying jobs for all. This emphasis on equality of opportunity, without explicitly stating it, put emphasis on the survival of the fittest ethos rather than equality and social justice. This, in turn, became a rationale for punishing and oppressing the unemployed poor as losers in the competitive job market.

The failure to acknowledge that persons would be displaced to the ranks of the unemployed and under-employed led to a backlash by threatened low-income, white males against the civil rights movement. It broke up the class struggle, i.e., the struggle between workers and the owners and managers of the means of production, by pitting low-income, white males against minorities and women. Many white males, for their defense, turned to the laissez-faire

25

conservatives under Reagan, who got over 60 percent of the white male vote and started a trend that has continued, except for the union vote, ever since. Particularly in the South the Republican Party became the party of the whites and the Democratic party of the African Americans. That phenomenon combined with the growing weakness of the union movement fostered the growing conservatism of the last quarter of the century.

The backlash against the civil rights movement took several forms:

- The opposition to affirmative action by those whites and others who feared they would be displaced.
- The war against poverty became a war against the poor, with tremendous racial and ethnic overtones. Blaming the victim was used and resulted in punitive and oppressive attacks on social welfare benefits to the unemployed poor and deprived many recipients of the human right to basic sustenance.
- The concentration of drug enforcement activities was disproportionately applied to the poor, and resulted in high rates of incarceration, especially for African Americans, that persists to this day.

A response calls for increased consciousness about the interplay between an emphasis on equality of opportunity and equality of condition. An emphasis on the ethos of survival of the fittest creates a fear of being displaced into the ranks of the losers, with a threat to human rights and survival. One can hardly blame those threatened for opposing this increased competition. There will be less resistance to civil rights and equality of opportunity if the "losers" have at least their basic human rights protected. Social justice must provide for the rights of all. Those interested in their own civil rights must avoid an attitude of "we do not care" about the problems of unemployment and poor-paying jobs as long as they do not include us. This challenges those interested in social justice to emphasize full employment, economic growth, higher wages and policies to strengthen the labor movement. The focus on civil rights and affirmative action must be seen as accompanying this, not replacing it. Civil rights are far easier to affect in an economy of expanding opportunities.

Affirmative action should be applied to all those who are qualified and not become a form of reverse discrimination by displacing those who are qualified in favor of the unqualified. Race relations are vastly improved when both whites and African Americans work together in the labor movement and elsewhere in the struggle for social justice. Notably Jesse Jackson, along with other civil rights leaders, has seen the basic struggle as a class struggle, as this is where the votes are; and that the conservatives are winning through a divide-and-rule strategy.

Chapter 3

The Employment, Wages, and Labor Relations Systems

The Struggle in Increasing Employment and Economic Growth

The most basic system regarding social justice concerns is the functioning of the economy to provide employment and wages. Article 23 of the Universal Declaration of Human Rights (United Nations, 1948) states:

> "(1) Everyone has the right to work, to free choice of employment, to just and favorable conditions of work and to protection against unemployment. (2) Everyone, without any discrimination, has the right to equal pay for equal work. (3) Everyone who works has the right to just and favorable remuneration ensuring for himself and his family an existence worthy of human dignity, and supplemented, if necessary, by other means of social protection. (4) Everyone has the right to form and to join trade unions for the protection of his interests."

These objectives are best achieved by public and private policies that promote full employment and economic growth, and address unemployment, wages, working conditions and job security. Social justice is concerned not just with economic growth, but with the distribution of wealth and income. Central to this is the establishment of a full employment economy and a reduction in unemployment. Policies needed to accomplish this led to the federal Employment Act of 1946, which called for economic planning for full employment by means of expanding the federal budget when needed to create increased employment opportunities. The Act created the Council of Economic Advisors to advise the President as to spending and other policies to achieve full employment.

The Act, drawing on the teachings of John Maynard Keynes and others, was based on the macro-economic concept that considers the level of employment as a consequence of the aggregate demand for goods and services. It deals with the business cycle that is seen as the result of uneven economic growth due to an uneven level of investment. In times of recession the Employment Act seeks to stimulate the economy by increased expenditures financed mostly by deficit spending (Galbraith, 1996). This economic stimulus is seen as having a "pump-priming" effect, as money spent is re-spent to further increase demand. This relies largely on increased federal spending for public projects, and policies to aid private investment such as lowering interest rates. Another approach, quicker to implement, is to reduce income taxes for consumers so they have more money to spend. The use of increased governmental expenditures has the advantage of being targeted to areas where it is needed most. For example, during the Great Depression funds were provided for public housing projects in an effort to revive the slumping construction industry.

The use of deficit spending has troubled conservatives. It is basically a way of increasing public expenditures by increasing the money supply. If done with restraint, it will not generate inflation. It is financed by government bonds, which are seen as a very safe investment. The interest payments to the bondholders provide for such things as retirement incomes that help the economy. The burden of interest payments to bondholders depends on the relationship to national income and the tax base, so that it becomes less burdensome as the economy expands. Also, deficit reduction is a means of deflating the economy in boom times and thus reducing the threat of inflation.

Most economists, even those with conservative leanings, have supported the use of economic stimulus to pump-prime the economy into recovery. In 2009, the Obama administration launched an economic stimulus plan that consisted of expenditures for such things as aid to local governments to avoid layoffs of teachers and other public employees, infrastructure grants for highway and other means of transportation, and for the development of clean energy. Most economists agreed that the economic stimulus increased aggregate demand, slowed unemployment, and began economic improvement. However conservatives criticized it for not reducing unemployment fast enough, not providing more stimulus funds to the private economy, and for increasing the burden of debt.

Another means of aiding economic recovery is by promoting private investment. The most acceptable means of doing this is to use monetary policies, such as the Federal Reserve lowering interest rates. There will not be much investment in a downward spiral of decreasing demand regardless of low interest rates and other means of encouraging investment. To stimulate the economy, what must happen first is to begin an upward spiral and then provide aid for private investment in response to increased demand.

Many feel big businesses have substantial savings for investment in expansion that will provide new markets and lead to increased returns on investments. Thus there does not seem to be much need to lower interest rates or for tax breaks and other incentives to big businesses to aid investment.

Small businesses, however, rely on loans for investment and benefit from low interest rates. They can be helped by other incentives, such as a tax disregard on investments in real property and capital equipment for some years, to give the businesses time to build up a return on the investment. There seems to be a special need to aid venture capital investment to start a new line of business by providing grants, in addition to relying on loans that lenders might regard as too risky.

One main use of monetary policies is to control interest rates to curtail speculative investment in boom times, which could be followed by a big bust that would damage the functioning of the whole economy. This was the case with the housing boom at the beginning of the twenty-first century, when larger mortgages than borrowers could afford led to foreclosures that then led to the recession.

One of the best means of increasing employment through economic growth is to develop infrastructure services that serve all, including transportation, public utilities, health care and education. There are many opportunities for the use of public and private funds to develop and improve these services that can result in economic expansion and the reduction of unemployment. Paramount is the need for conservation of energy and the development of alternative sources of energy. Fast-evolving technology is attaining fuel efficiency through technologies like hybrid autos and better batteries (Rahm & Coggburn, 2007).

Another potential is to develop a high-speed rail system that could haul containers at speeds of at least 100 miles an hour. In such inter-modal operations, a train of 100 containers operated by a crew of two could take 100 trailers off the highway with an immense savings in fuel as well as greater safety, less wear and tear on highways and equipment, and more efficient use of manpower. There needs to be increased development of alternative energy sources, such as ethanol, use of renewable sources, and greater use of nuclear power, as well as cleaner coal-fired generators.

In the human service area, healthcare and education are an increasing part of the economy and an increasing source of employment. Expanding medical technology requires new equipment, expanded facilities and more trained staff, which also requires expanded public payments for health services. Hospitals, nursing homes and other health facilities are among the largest employers of minority women, which have moved many from poverty.

About 60 percent of those working in the service occupations are African American and Hispanic women (U.S. Bureau of Labor Statistic, 2011a). Economic development requires an expansion of high-tech education and training programs, particularly at the tertiary level, using increased public funds.

Much of the struggle for economic development has been over location, with various localities offering huge tax concessions for business prospects in competition with each other. How effective these have been is questionable. There are numerous factors affecting location, including land cost, level of wages, the supply of needed labor, proximity to markets, sources of supply, environmental protection and affordable housing for workers.

When a location offers a combination of these factors, businesses are apt to locate their regardless of tax concessions to do so. Tax concessions make even less sense in the case of suburban malls and other retail developments, where developers are willing to pay high prices for locations near markets they will use regardless of tax concessions.

These concessions only serve to deprive local governments of funds they need for more roads, police and fire services and a larger school population. Many states and localities granted tax concessions to businesses based on the promise of creating a certain number of new jobs. There have been countless cases where this has not happened, and many states threaten to end the tax concessions for those businesses that have not complied (Buss, 2001).

Rather than offering tax concessions to attract businesses, many advocate better use of state and regional planning to make optimum use of resources and other factors, such as environmental protection. That locates development where it is most needed for creating jobs and can be combined with redevelopment of needed infrastructure services that includes affordable housing.

The goals of social justice are furthered when economic planning is used to achieve a greater socio-economic mix. That makes communities more mindful of the needs of low income persons, and a socio- economic mix in schools has been shown to further more equal education as children learn from each other, and hence those with better educated parents help those that are not so advantaged (Kahlenberg, 2003).

A factor of increasing concern is the declining number of manufacturing jobs due to increasing automation and other labor-saving methods in manufacturing, and the increase of out-sourcing manufacturing to other countries where labor costs are much lower. The percent of employment in manufacturing among non-farm worker has declined dramatically since the 1950s (see Figure 3.1 on the next page).

Much of this decline represents a shift to labor-intensive service jobs, such as janitorial and maid services, health care aides, retail, financial, construction and transportation services. The wonder is that this has not caused greater economic problems, as most service jobs pay considerably less.

One consequence has been efforts to increase pay in these jobs to correspond more with manufacturing jobs. This is reflected in the higher cost of such things as construction, healthcare and education. Also there has been an increase in productivity in such areas as retailing by larger stores; financial services, through use of computers; and in transportation, through use of larger and faster trucks.

It is generally agreed that the loss of many middle income manufacturing jobs has reduced income and resulted in greater inequality, and that a strong manufacturing sector is essential to a strong national economy (Gittell & Rudokas, 2007). *CBIA*

Much of the decline in manufacturing jobs is due to outsourcing to other countries of the manufacturing of many items for sale in the U.S. Globalization can benefit domestic economies. One thought is that outsourcing to underdeveloped countries of low-wage production, such as textiles, produces income that can be spent for imports of capital-intensive, high-wage products, such as autos and motorcycles produced in more developed countries.

Examples are the success of the Japanese in developing Asian economies so they could sell high-wage manufactured products, and the European Union, where investment in manufacturing in Ireland, Spain, Portugal, Southern Italy and Eastern Europe has provided new markets for the industrial countries of Germany, France and Northern Italy to sell their high-wage products. The advancement of underdeveloped countries due to outsourcing from advanced industrial nations can be explained by the flying geese paradigm (Akamatsu, 1962). The flying geese model explains the industrialization process in three stages: import, production, and export. In the first stage, the follower economy, seeking development, imports foreign goods; in the second stage, production of the imported manufactured goods begins; and in the third stage, the local production produced in excess is exported. As follower economies import modern goods, the local market will expand, and in repeating the patterns of leading countries a follower country can

Figure 3.1

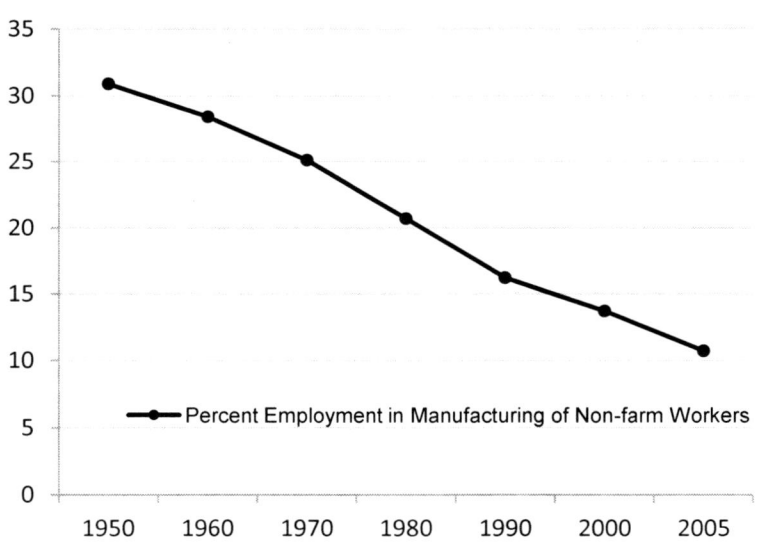

Percentage of Employment in Manufacturing of
Non-farm Workers by Decades
Source: U.S. Department of Labor, n.d.

34

catch up. There is increasing concern that too much outsourced work is done by sweatshops and child labor, especially in Asia and Central and South America, which is not helping these economies to grow (Arnold & Bowie, 2003).

These practices lead to greater profits for outsourcing companies but not for producing markets, like in the U.S., where produced items are more expensive. Many unions feel that this leads to unfair competition, and many of those concerned with social justice are pressing to impose the labor standards developed by the U.N. Many activists groups, especially on some college campuses, have tried to organize boycotts of goods produced overseas by sweatshops and child labor.

There are many products that require too much capital and skilled labor to be easily outsourced to underdeveloped countries. This includes aerospace, machinery and other high-tech items. Actions by General Electric (GE) in reorganizing provide an example of this. GE invested in the production of jet engines, diesel locomotives and generating equipment, resulting in tremendous value added and high profits per unit of production. This required a large capital investment, high skilled product development and production. Still there is concern that too many relatively high-wage manufacturing jobs are being outsourced at considerably lower wages.

There seems to be an increasing trend to outsource many high-wage unionized jobs, where the necessary skills can be found at much lower wages. This results in both increased profits, despite less productivity of foreign labor, and the decline of the dollar, which increases the cost of foreign labor. Laissez-faire conservatives justify this as a desirable use of the market economy, which levels the world by raising the standard of living of the underdeveloped nations. They view this as a "zero-sum" game, in which the standard of living of the underdeveloped world is raised at the expense of the high-wage developed world. Social liberals concerned with social justice realize that there is a global economy, and they want to see the standard of living raised in the underdeveloped world, but they also want the global economy to foster greater equality within these nations (Weller, Scott, & Hersh, 2003). They believe more equality lessens internal violence and that world trade fosters world peace. They want these economies to grow faster than those of the developed world, but believe that this can happen without depressing the economies of the developed world. Hence, they feel that outsourcing needs to be curtailed by trade agreements, restricting imports or negotiating protective tariffs, so that capital-intensive and high-value items are produced at higher wages and labor standards. They want to extend this to restrict the import of high value-added parts to be used in domestic assembly. Advocates have also urged that all government contracts be examined to prevent outsourcing jobs, especially high- wage jobs.

The Struggle for Job Security

An important challenge in the struggle for social justice is the provision of job security. Clearly one of the main tasks in working for social justice is to provide for employment opportunities and the maintenance of income when employment income is terminated due to the functioning of the economy, illness, disability or retirement. This calls for the provision of unemployment benefits, paid sick leave benefits, retirement, and disability benefits. These benefits will be discussed at length in the chapters that follow.

The 2007 recession points to the need to have a stabilized economy that does not feature periods of economic boom followed by periods of economic decline with negative effects on employment. Hence central to employment security is the use of fiscal and monetary policies to provide for economic stability, as discussed previously. Another possible action that needs to be given real consideration is avoiding layoffs in periods of recession, which further result in the loss of income and contribute to the downward spiral of the economy. As an alternative to layoffs, employers need to be encouraged to reduce employment costs by reducing the hours of employment of most employees, and reducing the salaries of most employees according to their ability to manage with reduced income. Reports indicate that the Japanese have made a real effort to maintain employment in periods of recession, which helped to reduce the severity of periods of recession (Gross & Tran, 2003).

A disturbing trend is the loss of job security in a dynamic labor market. This is characterized by changes in the nature and location of the production of goods and services, resulting in many layoffs. Shifts in job skills required due to the computer age and other new forms of technology have led to the replacement of many older workers with newer workers who have the necessary skills, often at lower wages and with fewer employee benefits (Fisher, 2007). In an effort to promote efficiency and lower labor costs, employers have implemented a new strategy termed "slash-and-burn tactics," with various departments told to lay off a specified number of workers, and forced to decide which workers to cut (Cascio, 2002). Some employers, for security reasons, discharge employees on the spot without any warning, and have security personnel help them take their possessions and turn in their keys and badges. It is hard to imagine a more cruel way to treat employees. The result has been a loss of job security, with more and more jobs no longer including seniority protection. Seniority protection is what unions have long fought for, and with the decline of union membership there is less support. These layoffs seem an unjust response, especially to terminate a longtime employee short of retirement and with little prospects of finding employment at the former wage. Many employers have recognized this and have offered termination benefits, including benefits for early retirement (Fisher, 2007).

This situation demands responses. One is to make it easier for unions to organize and bargain for seniority protection and for termination benefits. Faculty organizations and unions in colleges and universities have long made academic tenure one of their main causes. One might hope that someday a federal law would be passed requiring employers to provide seniority protection to a majority of their employees. This would require a clear definition as to whom can be classified as a temporary employee for whom seniority protection and employee benefits do not apply. Employers should be required to give notice at least two weeks prior to termination, except in a situation requiring immediate action. Furthermore, discharged employees should have the right to a hearing before an arbitrator in instances where they feel that they have been unfairly terminated. Based on seniority, employees should receive retirement benefits, early retirement, 401K plans, or IRA payments that would aid early retirement. In a climate of economic hardship this is not easy to achieve but should not be discarded. The Japanese, who are noted for their efficiency and high productivity, would rarely consider disregarding seniority protection, as they see the value of employee security and high morale (Takahashi, 1990).

The Struggle for Equality in Wages, Salaries and Working Conditions

Basic to social justice is the struggle for greater equality in wages, salaries, and working conditions. It is here where the dynamics of social dominance and the labor market make the struggle most intense, and where the basics need to be understood and the issues clarified (Kuttner, 1999). One of the most basic issues is that of economic growth versus economic equity, or the size of the pie versus how it is cut up. From the point of view of social dominance and the market economy, many would argue that one must come at the expense of the other. They would argue that without the incentive for social dominance there is no motivation for growth; that higher wages increase costs, reduce profits and lower the incentive to invest; and that to pay persons more than they would earn in a competitive labor market is to reward inefficiency and hence fail to make optimum use of resources in growth and development.

Those looking at this from the perspective of social justice would argue that there is little evidence that growth and equality are an "either-or" proposition. In fact most underdeveloped countries are characterized by great inequality, particularly between the owners of property and paid labor. There are many examples of capitalist countries that have achieved a high level of growth while, at the same time—through combined use of market economy concepts and public policies—have achieved greater equality in the distribution of income. One of the most basic concepts is that real economic growth depends on passing along greater productivity in the form of higher wages, which can be increased due to lower unit costs without increasing prices. This situation thus provides greater spending power for the purchase of more goods and services. Advocates of social justice point out that this provides an economic growth dividend that can be transferred to support social welfare programs that will lead to poverty reduction and the enhancement of the whole economy (Rodrik, 2000; Stewart, 2000). Hence, this calls for public policies that increase productivity, such as educating and training more technicians and providing tax relief that leads to more investment in increasing productivity.

Many economists using macro-economic analysis agree that higher wages negotiated by unions are a factor in economic growth, and that generally this has overcome whatever negatives have occurred due to less profits and higher labor costs. Research has found that high income inequality causes nations to have lower rates of economic growth due to the lack of purchasing power (Kuttner, 1992).

Another basic concept is that wages are as much related to where one works as to what one does. Here the concept is that the value of labor is related to how much a unit of labor adds to value.

Hence a worker making a high priced machine tool is entitled to earn more than, for example, a worker making shoes. Another example is that an attorney earning $200 an hour can easily afford to pay a secretary $20 an hour, as it is a small percent of the value of the service rendered, whereas a wage of $20 an hour to a secretary would be too large in an office where most other workers earn less than $25 an hour. It is this concept of value added that has great effect on what the market system pays in wages and, hence, is the source of great inequality in wages. This is best illustrated in the low pay provided in labor-intensive employment that produces cheap products, such as the harvesting of many farm products. What needs to be considered is the passing on of greater productivity vertically to the less productive parts of the process. Thus, in food processing greater productivity could be passed on in higher wages for less productive harvesting by minimum wage coverage and labor union organizing in agriculture, without raising food prices. This would greatly enhance social justice objectives of economic equality.

Also related to this are the high costs of labor in labor-intensive employments, if they are to pay wages comparable to those in capital-intensive employments. This is especially true in human service employment, such as education and healthcare, where there are clear limits on how much labor-saving equipment can replace human labor, and in which the increased need for high-skilled labor in these areas further increases labor costs. The result is soaring labor costs in these settings that put great strains on the need for increased funding. This need for funding produces a double challenge; teachers and health workers must turn to the public sector to fund increasing labor costs, and this forces unions in these areas to spend efforts in getting increased public appropriations. One of the biggest challenges to social justice is that wages, especially for low paid workers, are falling behind the increased cost of essentials, such as housing, energy, and medical care, causing a real decline in their standard of living, hurting the economy and increasing inequality. Several factors explain the increasing inequality. The main factors are the loss of manufacturing jobs and the resulting decline in the labor movement, and the outsourcing of many high paid jobs and competition from the importation of products produced by low paid labor.

There are two main systems for achieving greater equality in wages, salaries, and working conditions other than what is provided through the market system. The first is through public regulation on wages, salaries, employee benefits, and working conditions; and the second is through trade unions and other employee organizations, in what can be called the labor relations system. In public regulations a key challenge is to raise the minimum wage so that, as expressed in the U.N. Universal Declaration of Human Rights (1948), "Everyone who works has the right to just and favorable remuneration ensuring for himself and his family an existence worthy of human dignity." This declaration has often been put as "the right to a living wage." The level of minimum wages has been of concern. The federal minimum wage had tended to be about half of the average wages and has fallen to less than 40 percent. With the decline in the average wages in recent years, the minimum wage is even less adequate (Social Security Online, 2010; United States Department of Labor, 2010). Minimum wages have never been high enough by themselves to lift persons over the poverty line.

Raising minimum wages puts some pressure on raising the wage scale in occupations to maintain the proper differences between the level of skill and responsibility required. Some argue that wage increases are just passed on in increased prices so that there is no overall benefit. However, the price increases are spread over all consumers, so that the increase in prices is slight and the gains to those who do not earn a decent living wage are immense. It is also argued that if wages are raised some employees will have to be laid off in order to hold down labor costs, which assumes that there is a lot of surplus unneeded labor. In response to this, economists point out that increased wages are an incentive to increase productivity, and that increased wages result in increased demand that, in turn, increases employment (Cascio, 2002). Research by Card and Krueger (1994), in fact, shows that minimum wages have reduced poverty and raised employment. Clearly minimum wage protection at all levels—federal, state and local—needs to be extended to farm labor and all forms of employment.

Wage levels are also affected by low-wage competition, by importing low-paid foreign labor to fill jobs and by the importation of goods produced by cheap labor. The importation of cheap labor can be partly dealt with through higher minimum wages and, especially, by establishing quotas on immigration. These actions are resisted by employers who want a large pool of available cheap labor to make it easier to fill low-wage jobs, and by ethnic groups that feel excluded because they are a source of cheap labor. There is also a need to enforce international labor standards against exploitation of labor through sweatshops and child labor. There further needs to be pressure on countries to give workers the right to organize trade unions, which is a tenet of the Universal Declaration of Human Rights. As has been pointed out, there is a need to negotiate trade agreements that protect high-wage jobs from competition from cheap foreign labor.

The goals of social justice in line with the Declaration of Human Rights call for increasing the number of employers paying a living wage, which provides families with the necessities for a decent standard of living. Research has shown the minimum wages pay only about a third of what is regarded as a living wage. For example, Wider Opportunities for Women (Pearce & Brooks, 2002) determined that in Miami a single parent with two young children, in order to be completely self sufficient, would need an annual income of almost $40,000, and that the minimum wage was only a third of this amount. Bargaining for a living wage has long been one of the major goals of the labor movement. Here a factor has been the growing political power of the public service unions, especially in cities, where together with the support of liberal advocacy groups, women's organizations, and fellow travelers of the same race and ethnicity, they have passed ordinances establishing living wages for government employees. In recent years about 140 cities and local governments have approved a living wage for municipal employees, and many of these have also required it of contractors doing business with those local governments (Olson & Steinman, 2005). In order to forestall breaking unions by contracting out jobs at less than union wages, unions have had some success in requiring contractors with state and federal governments to pay prevailing wages. There have been efforts to require state governments to pay a living wage to all state employees, which have been defeated by conservatives concerned about reducing the costs of government. Hence, promoting a living wage largely depends on the strength of unions with some help from liberal groups and the women's movement. Success will depend on what can be done to strengthen the union movement.

With state and local governments facing continuing large declines in revenues, unions are forced to make wage concessions; and the chances of getting governments to pay a living wage appear slim. Instead of increasing wages, there will be continued efforts to subsidize low wages when needed. There are subsidies for dependent children through federal and state earned income tax credits, and for food stamps, medical care, and housing. These may need to be expanded in the face of lower incomes and rising costs. There also needs to be better protection of hours and working conditions, as are embodied in the federal Fair Labor Standards Act and Occupational Safety and Health Act. The George W. Bush administration tried to weaken the time-and-a-half for overtime provisions of the Fair Labor Standards Act, and the 2010 West Virginia coal mine disaster points to the need for greater occupational safety.

The Labor Relations System

Article 23, Section 4, of the Declaration of Human Rights (United Nations, 1948) states "Everyone has the right to form and to join trade unions for the protection of his interests." Trade unions are one of the most vital elements in the struggle for social justice. They are the main source for achieving fair and equal wages, for promoting safe and decent working conditions, and for protecting job security through seniority systems and workers' rights to employee benefits. Unions have also been the main constituency for promoting social welfare legislation. For example, unions were mainly responsible for the passage of the Medicare and Medicaid legislation of the 1960s. Hence, all those involved in the struggle for social justice need to be strong supporters of the trade union movement and support the right of workers to form trade unions.

Historically the trade union movement goes back to medieval guilds that controlled apprenticeships, skill standards, wages, and working conditions. The guilds led to unions based on definite skills, especially in the construction, crafts, and transportation employments that came together under the American Federation of Labor (AFL). With the development of manufacturing, which involved a combination of many skills, unions were organized more on industrial lines that greatly expanded the union movement. The industrial union movement flourished during the 1930s, which saw the formation of the Congress of Industrial Organizations (CIO). The CIO was comprised of large, powerful unions that included miners and garment, steel, auto, electrical and aero-space workers. The union movement was a major force behind the New Deal of the Roosevelt administration, which produced significant labor and social legislation that greatly furthered the cause of social justice.

Most significant was the passage of the federal Labor Relations Act, which offered many labor protections and established fair labor practices. Notably, workers could not be fired for joining a union and employers were required to hold elections to certify a union as a collective bargaining unit and to bargain in good faith. A government mediation service was set up to facilitate the settling of labor disputes, especially when strikes were involved. Unions winning elections were authorized to establish a union shop, in which all employees in covered employments were required to join that union and have part of their pay deducted—"checked off"— for union dues. Another significant development was the passage of the federal Fair Labor Standards Act, which established the minimum wage and the forty-hour week with time- and-a-half pay for overtime that greatly increased workers' earnings. Most state governments passed similar legislation to cover employments not engaged in inter-state commerce.

The labor movement flourished during the post-war period of the 1950s and 1960s, which saw the merger of the AFL and the CIO. Relatively full employment and wage increases resulted in increased equality of income and enabled many industrial workers to achieve middle class status. Unfortunately, the post-war boom came to an end in the 1970s and led to a dramatic decline in the labor movement. That has continued ever since, and has been a real factor in the growing political strength of the laissez-faire conservatives. From 1980 to 2005, there has been a drastic drop in the percent of all salaried and wage workers who are union members and work in covered employment (see Table 3.1).

Table 3.1
Union Membership and Coverage

Year	% of Union Members	% of Workers Covered by a Union
1980	23.3	26.1
1990	16.3	18.6
2000	13.6	15
2010	11.9	13.1

Source: For the years 1980-2000, Hirsch, Macpherson, & Vroman, 2001; For the year 2010, U.S. Bureau of Labor Statistics, 2011d

Much of this decline has been due to the shift from manufacturing to service employment and the outsourcing and contracting out of many union jobs. Union organizing in manufacturing plants is relatively easier when all employees work together, and where a strike or job action is easier to organize. Service jobs such as janitors and clerical workers tend to be both more spread out and intermingled with management. It is also easier to contract out service jobs, such as office cleaning and computer services; and efforts to organize the contractors are met with the response that increased wages would result in contracts lost to a lower bidder paying lower wages. Also, the fewer members the union movement has the weaker it becomes. When there are a lot of nonunion workers who can be hired, it becomes much easier to break strikes and harder to stop the hiring of nonunion workers in such areas as construction. Even more significant is the loss of union votes needed for the passage and continuing support of labor and social legislation. The most obvious example of loss of political power was in 1981, when President Reagan fired all the air traffic controllers who were on strike. This has made it easier to fire strikers ever since.

With a weakened labor movement, employers have been able to be more intimidating, so that it becomes harder to win union elections. Also, conservative forces have been able to defeat most legislation to aid organizing submitted by unions, even in states where the legislature is controlled by liberals. To turn this decline around in the current climate will be difficult. Unions have been seeking legislation to make it easier to organize collective bargaining units by getting a majority of workers to sign a petition requesting the recognition of a union as a bargaining agent rather than having to win an election. This is controversial, as many agree that the union movement should be more democratic. If workers, for example, are to be required to join a union that is certified as a collective bargaining agent, this should be done by the union winning an election that involves use of a secret ballot.

The National Labor Relations Board and state boards need to be more committed to the right of employees to join unions as provided in the Universal Declaration of Human rights, which have eroded in the years of conservative governments. Elections must be made fairer by requiring fair labor practices, such as giving workers the right to have an equal chance to present their case and by restricting employers from requiring workers to attend meetings in which they make threats against unionization without the union being there to present its side. To achieve this protection, actions such as the following are required:

- More elections need to be supervised by the National Labor Relations Board or state boards.
- There should be provision for a more rapid election process, as often this is stretched out over a year with the establishment of a collective bargaining process taking still longer.
- There needs to be more action to prevent employees from being discharged or penalized for union activity.
- Employees should be eligible for unemployment benefits when on strike after a waiting period.
- In settings where a strike would jeopardize needed public services, such as a police strike or a teachers strike, there need to be provision for compulsory arbitration.
- There needs to be legislation to require that strikers be rehired when strikes are over.

Many of these proposals for legislation are found in Canada, where around 30 percent of the labor force is unionized. Employers will threaten that higher wages and more employee benefits will give their nonunion competitors an advantage. Hence, an approach is to pass legislation to require that all employers provide many of the benefits now provided in many unionized employments. This would establish more equality among employments and diminish efforts by employers to reduce many employee benefits in the face of rising costs. The most obvious need would be to establish a government financed universal health program or require employers to offer employee benefits. Employers could be required to offer paid sick leave, seniority protection and even contribute to employee retirement plans.

The contracting out of union jobs to nonunion contractors has been an effective way to break the union movement. Badly needed is legislation to restrict who can be called an independent contractor and not an employee. A factor would be how much the employee worked independently without having to coordinate with paid workers and without the continuous supervision of a paid employee. In dealing with contracting of union jobs at low wages, the need is for national, state, and local legislation to require that government contracts pay a living wage, or wages comparable to union wages. All of these proposals will be strongly opposed by employers and employer organizations, such as chambers of commerce, which can use tremendous lobbying efforts. To be effective, counter efforts cannot be done by the union movement alone, and will require extensive support from all those forces committed to social justice.

Chapter 4
The Social Welfare System

Basics of the Social Welfare System

The welfare state is composed of public social welfare programs that deal with the needs of the unemployed, retirees, the sick and disabled, and families for economic security and a decent standard of living, including the provision of food, housing, medical care (including rehabilitation and longterm care), and necessary social services. The main tasks of the social welfare system are to further social justice by providing a means for meeting basic human rights, and to further equality, social security and a decent standard of living for all. There are many ways to discuss the social welfare system. For purposes of policy action, it is best to use the concept of a nonmarket exchange. This concept is central to the concept of welfare and refers to any provision of income, goods and services that is not the result of paying for one's labor or sale of one's goods and services in a market exchange. Such welfare payments can be in the form of public and private benefits given to eligible persons; employee benefits, in addition to wages, that are termed occupational welfare; and in the form of tax concessions, deductions and credits—to help either provide more tax-free income or lower the costs of goods and services—that is termed fiscal welfare (Titmuss, 1958). Social welfare programs are part of mutual support systems, of which barn raisings and volunteer fire departments are examples. Social welfare programs provide income, goods and services to those who are judged as needing them, such as retirees, the sick and disabled, the unemployed and under-employed and those with dependents to care for.

Social welfare in accordance with the concepts of social justice should not be just concerned with the elimination of poverty,

49

but also with the provision of basic human rights, such as expressed in Article 25 of the Universal Declaration of Human Rights (United Nations, 1948):

> "Everyone has the right to a standard of living adequate for the health and well-being of himself and of his family, including food, clothing, housing and medical care and the necessary social services, and the right to security in the event of unemployment, sickness, disability and widowhood, old age or other lack of livelihood in circumstances beyond his control."

That calls for higher standards than the poverty line established by the federal government. The federal poverty line was originally based on what is called the economy food budget. This dealt with the minimum that one had to spend for food in order to have adequate nutrition. The budget is then multiplied by three, on the basis that one needs to spend a third of his budget on food. This figure has been adjusted each year for inflation. With the costs of housing, energy and medical care rising faster than inflation, the federal poverty line is not a realistic indicator. An income above the poverty line is no longer adequate to enable a person to be able to afford such things as housing and medical care. That is revealed by the fact that the maximum income to be eligible for assistance in these areas is usually set at a multiple of the poverty line, such as 200 percent of poverty.

An emphasis on eliminating poverty rather than on human rights puts a focus on the poor as a separate group rather than on those whose income is too low for the provision of some human rights. This leads to a "blaming the victim" approach to poverty. Some books on social deviancy include the poor as deviants, and there has been discussion of "the culture of poverty" that presents the norms and values of the poor as the cause of the problem rather than due to the functioning of the market economy. Further, the response to poverty depends greatly on how compassionate one feels for the poor, or how deserving they are seen, rather than on their human rights. How compassionate one is often depends on how much one has an identity with the poor based on similar attributes such as race, ethnicity, age, sex, place of residence, or similar circumstances, such as unemployment or disability.

Rather than measure poverty according to what people need to afford basic essentials, a better measurement to achieve equality would be to set the poverty standard as some percentage of median family income. This is done in the federal rent supplement program, which entitles families to a rent supplement whose income is a percent of median family income—an approach that makes it more redistributive, and a means for having more equality in the distribution of income.

Ideally, a statement on basic human rights for a decent standard of living and for economic security, such as in the Universal Declaration, should be included in the federal and state constitutions. A survey of state constitutions showed that, for the most part, this was limited to the right to an education (Wronka, 1991). The right to an education in the Connecticut state constitution was used in the *Sheff v. O'Neill* case, which decided that persons were entitled to an equal education, and hence action was taken for schools to be racially integrated to achieve equality (Connecticut Judicial Branch, 1999). There was a similar effort to deal with welfare cutoffs by amending the Connecticut state constitution to say that children were entitled to basic sustenance. That might have succeeded if there had been a better-organized effort. However, the ethic of the market economy does not deal with the right to a decent standard of living, economic security or a living wage, and instead emphasizes the opportunity and responsibility to compete in the labor market in the struggle for self-sufficiency. Hence, it will be difficult to change public policies to include economic rights as a part of human rights.

In providing for human rights, a basic concept of social welfare programs is the entitlement of all eligible persons to benefits, and not just to a charitable distribution based on the willingness of persons to give. This concept leads to another basic concept—that charity does not displace justice. Recipients of charity have no entitlement rights and are dependent on the beneficence of givers, which creates a dependency that enhances the dominance of the giver over the receiver, and that serves as a means for enhancing the social esteem of the giver. Another concept of entitlement is that needs should be fully met as long as they exist, and not by some token assistance or on a temporary and emergency basis.

One of the most basic distinctions in the provision of social welfare benefits is whether they are provided in the form of cash benefits or what are called "in-kind" payments for specified goods and services, such as food stamps, and for medical care. The main reason given for cash benefits is the concept of consumer sovereignty, i.e., that consumers should get to choose where to spend their income according to what they regard as most needed. This is the argument given for the adoption of a negative income tax, which provides a cash payment to those whose income is below what they need for a decent standard of living. Extremists would have cash benefits replace almost all benefits such as food stamps, medical expense payments and various income tax deductions. However, in the final analysis social welfare programs are not about consumer sovereignty but, rather, about assuring that people are provided with basic essentials such as food, housing and medical care, and that the benefits should reflect the costs of these items. Furthermore, consumer sovereignty can serve as a means for human oppression when benefits are cut on the basis that the beneficiary is most equipped to decide what he or she can best do without. For example, welfare grants used to be determined by budgeting for actual expenses such as rent and utility costs. This has been replaced by flat grants that vary only by family size and do not consider actual rent and other costs. This has been justified on the basis of consumer sovereignty; but when it is not enough to cover necessary expenses, it is a form of human oppression. This is illustrated by increases in homelessness because recipients did not receive enough in their grant to pay for rent, food, and other essentials. Payments for specific expenses have the advantage of assuring that the benefits are actually spent on the need for which they are intended. They also have the support of the providers, such as farmers, and medical providers, including physicians, hospitals, and nursing homes. Bankers and the real estate industry similarly benefit by tax deductions on interest payments for mortgages.

A basic consideration in the provision of social welfare benefits is the means of determining eligibility. One means is to provide the benefit or service universally to all regardless of wealth or income. The best example is the provision of public education to all children regardless of family income. Many countries provide medical care for all that is paid out of public funds in what is called a single-payer system. Some countries provide universal pension benefits to all, and other countries pay a universal child allowance for all children on the basis that all families need extra income if they have children. Other countries, such as New Zealand, pay a universal allowance to all physically disabled people. Universal benefits can also be provided as a form of fiscal welfare by giving all persons a tax credit for children or for the payment of medical insurance premiums.

Universal benefits have the obvious advantage of treating all persons equally and, hence, are a major means for gaining social equality. This is best experienced when in public school the children of the very rich sit next to children on welfare, or when a rich person follows a low-income person into an operating room. When high-income persons receive these benefits and also get cash benefits for children or a universal tax credit, they are more likely to support paying progressive or proportional income taxes and, hence, it is a form of redistribution based on who pays, not on who receives. The problem with universal benefits is that they are costly, particularly when they pay cash benefits to high-income persons who do not need them. The result is often that universal benefits, such as pensions and children's allowances, are reduced, so that they are less adequate to meet the needs of low-income persons, while higher-income persons can afford to supplement them.

Another form of provision of benefits is through social insurance systems that pay benefits to all recipients regardless of income, in compensation for loss of income or increased costs due to occurrence of a covered situation such as death, retirement, illness, disability or unemployment. Social insurance is a means of mutual risk-sharing through contributions to a special insurance fund out of which benefits are paid. That is an effective method of dealing with the problem of paying benefits to persons that are not earned in the marketplace, as beneficiaries have paid a contribution into the insurance fund by taxes or premium payments from either their earnings or the earnings of spouses, parents or relatives. Sharing risks through insurance is a more effective way to provide protection rather than having individuals save for what might be a very significant loss or cost. This has led to the creation of a large insurance industry.

Social insurance by governments provides for all persons who are covered, usually based on a payroll tax system—typically a percentage of their income—that assures all those covered get benefits that they may not be able to afford or get from private insurance. Since all are included, social insurance shares risks more effectively than private insurance, which often has the problem of being sought out by high-risk people, especially those with health problems. This results in higher costs and creates a need to exclude high-risk persons despite their urgent need for coverage.

Payroll taxes tend to be regressive, in that they tax lower incomes at a larger percentage. This, in turn, makes the programs less a matter of the class struggle as working people pay for their own benefits. However, an advantage of a public system is that it can more easily be redistributive by paying a larger proportion of previous earnings to low income persons, as is done in the U.S. Social Security system. It is generally agreed that a social insurance system is more efficient than private insurance, as it has the benefit of high volume that lowers administrative costs, avoids having to pay salespeople and for marketing costs, and earns enough profit to pay an adequate return to the stockholders.

The fact that social insurance benefits go to all, regardless of income, and that the benefits are paid by contributions from beneficiaries, has made social insurance politically very popular. This was illustrated by opposition encountered by the George W. Bush administration in its efforts to allow beneficiaries of Social Security to convert a portion of their payroll taxes to a personal savings account program. There have been proposals to extend social insurance to such things as a divorce and separation by providing fatherless child insurance; but the basic concept of insurance is that it should not cover things that people would willfully seek, and there would be the obvious concern that this would lead to increases in marital breakup. Yet it would be interesting to experiment to determine how extensive this would be.

Social welfare benefits can also be "means tested," with eligibility based on not having enough income or other means to pay for what are regarded as needed essentials. This requires setting an income and asset level above which one is not entitled to benefits that is often measured against the costs of what is needed. Means-tested programs have the advantage of lowering costs, as they are provided only to the needy and, hence, hold down taxes, which makes them popular with laissez faire conservatives. One advantage is that eligibility levels can be more easily manipulated in response to greater need and higher costs. An example is the need to increase income limits for eligibility for healthcare costs in response to rising prices, which has made healthcare less affordable to an increasing number of low-income persons. The negative aspect is that the means testing separates the haves from the have-nots, who lack the power of numbers and socio-economic status.

Thus they become easy scapegoats for punitive and oppressive cuts in benefits. It has fostered a "blaming the victim" response to poverty and unemployment rather than changing the social-economic structure, in order to eliminate unemployment and low-income jobs (Daly, 1996). Cuts in benefits also serve the social dominance needs of the haves who want to increase the social distance between themselves and welfare recipients, whom they label as undeserving. That is further enhanced when the recipients are perceived as disproportionately representing a minority group characterized by race, ethnicity, religion or other features, such as illegal drug use.

The Struggle Between the Private Market and Social Welfare Systems

The struggle for social justice through the social welfare system basically involves a struggle with opposing concepts of justice in the market economy. This conflict is well illustrated in a biblical parable of a landowner who goes out at various hours of the day to hire unemployed laborers to work in the fields, and at the end of the day pays all workers the same regardless of how long they worked. Those who have worked all day in the heat of the sun protest, but the landowner replies that he has done them no harm, as he paid them what he had agreed to and they should not object to his being generous to the others who worked less. This shows that the justice of the marketplace is one of exchange, in this case one of receiving wages in exchange for the number of hours worked. By contrast social justice is about human rights, in this case the rights of the unemployed and underemployed to a decent standard of living.

Social welfare benefits are paid to the needy as a matter of right in a nonmarket exchange. Thus it is upsetting to the justice of the marketplace when people receive various social welfare benefits that they did not earn (Piven & Cloward, 1993). What is especially upsetting is that there is no incentive for a worker to take a low-paying, dirty, or unsafe job if an unemployed person can get social welfare benefits for his basic sustenance without working. This problem is as old as the welfare system. Even in the Middle Ages there were concerns about helping the so-called sturdy beggar who was able to work.

In the nineteenth century, when the labor market became more developed, there was the concept of "less eligibility," i.e., that the lot of the nonworking poor should not be better than that of the lowest paid laborer. This led to punitive and oppressive welfare policies, the principal one being taking care of the long time poor in almshouses and "poor farms," which resembled jails, where they were put to work for their sustenance without pay. A basic reform of the Social Security Act of 1935 was the requirement that public assistance benefits in the federally aided categories be in the form of what was called "outdoor relief" to persons in their own homes.

It has been said that the welfare benefits for the poor tend to be a degradation ceremony, the audience of which is the low-paid laborer, which leads to the observation that most programs for the poor are poor programs. The problem of public assistance payments to the able-bodied has continued to plague the welfare system. One recent emphasis has been on work for relief, which has been termed "workfare." It requires recipients to work for their benefits without pay on some community service project. More recently some able-bodied recipients without dependents who receive benefits under the state and local general assistance program have been cut off entirely, and provided only with food stamps and essential medical care. Welfare cutoffs were even extended to employable mothers with dependent children in the so- called "welfare reform act," the Personal Responsibility and Work Opportunity Reconciliation Act passed by the U.S. Congress in 1996. This act established a five-year time limit on benefits to the employable and allowed states to set even lower benefits. Under the Poor Law that dates back to colonial times, the basic needs of food, clothing and shelter had usually been provided, even if they were in an institution.

The definition of human oppression needs to include depriving persons of human rights, such as the economic right to basic sustenance. There were a few efforts to take care of some of the welfare cutoffs by dealing with emergencies such as homelessness, but studies showed that many families and individuals who were cut off suffered real deprivation. Those who did find jobs found mostly very low-paying or part-time work and did not escape poverty (Stuart & Bok, 2003). There is almost no evidence that this cutoff resulted in filling jobs that would not otherwise have been filled and hence reduce unemployment. Thus, it can best be understood as an example of the politics of oppression, which unifies all the rest—including low-paid workers and the wealthy—around oppressing the poor who become powerless scapegoats. The esteem of low-paid workers is raised, not by lifting them up but by pushing the unemployed poor down.

Hence, one could visit the concentration camp at Auschwitz and see the shoes displayed of the children put to death there, and say to one's self, "I cannot understand why this happened." What we are doing to the children cut off from welfare is in the same spirit. Sadly there is a lot of evidence that the politics of oppression works. It clearly helped to unify the Germans behind the Nazis, and here in the U.S., where the poor are perceived as mostly African American and Hispanics, it has attracted a lot of white non-Hispanic low-income persons, especially males, to vote with the conservatives.

Though the laissez-faire conservatives agree that the poor are entitled to some safety-net protection, many would confine this to providing only that which is necessary to sustain life, such as food and essential medical care. They would view the social welfare system as a residual backup system that most persons would never need (Abramovitz, 1986). This residual approach tends to treat problems such as homelessness as temporary emergencies rather than as an ongoing problem due to the inability to pay rent. It also often resorts in token gestures such as providing rent subsidies to a few drastic cases, rather than as an entitlement right to all those in need.

Another response is to advocate the use of private charity. This is the main basis of the faith-based social service programs advocated by the George W. Bush Administration, which would provide some aid to churches to help the poor, with no concept that this would provide for basic human rights of the needy. The provision of private charity is usually inadequate to meet more than a portion of needs, and it is dependent on the willingness to give, not on the rights of the recipient. Most research makes it clear that charity mainly serves to establish givers as moral, caring persons and to enhance their prestige and superiority, resulting in the receiver becoming dependent on them (Glazer & Konrad, 1996; Hernandez-Murillo & Roisman, n.d.; Johnson, 2011).

There is the concept of what has been called "mystification" that can be applied to the practice of charitable giving, insofar as a social hierarchy is created where the relationship between a superior and inferior is maintained. Those in need rely on the giver for charity, so the social inequality continues and social order is maintained (Cohen, 1969).

The residual model also sees unemployment and low wages as largely the fault of the worker who, in the survival of the fittest ethos, lost out in the competitive struggle for good paying jobs. It further expects the individuals and families to be self-sufficient, save or purchase private annuities for retirement, and save and purchase private insurance protection for loss of income due to disability, death of a parent, and for needed medical care. A part of consumer sovereignty is seen as deciding how much one should put aside for savings or for the purchase of private insurance. All of this is seen as a function of the market system that is distorted, when persons receive benefits from the public social welfare system without having to provide for their own economic security from their own income.

Advocates of social justice see the social welfare system not as a residual backup to the market system but, rather, as a necessary social institution standing aside of the market economy and fulfilling certain functions basic to achieving the objectives of social justice. This is well expressed in the term "welfare state," which sees the provision of social welfare services as one of the most basic functions of public policy. The social welfare system has had to accommodate to the concern about providing income and services that are not provided in the market in exchange for labor. The most common method of dealing with this, which is found in most federal and federally-aided welfare programs, is to categorize programs to exclude able-bodied employable persons. The best example is the federal Old Age, Survivors, and Disability Insurance (OASDI) program, targeted to children and the retired aged, who are outside the labor force. Disability benefits are restricted to the permanently and totally disabled, who are clearly outside of the labor force.

Another method of dealing with the labor market is to provide universal benefits, such as children's allowances or income tax deductions for children, to all families regardless of income or work status, which avoids distinguishing between the working and unemployed poor. A similar method is to use social insurance, such as OASDI and unemployment compensation, where benefits are paid from a special fund to which employees have contributed by a payroll tax on their wages. A further device is to supplement low wages and income by the provision of supplementary benefits, such as food stamps, housing supplements and medical care, to the working poor, not just to the unemployed.

The English Poor Law of 1601 that led to the establishment of the social welfare system included the provision that the able-bodied be put to work. This has been done, many times on a somewhat hit-or-miss basis, for the able-bodied, unemployed poor. Especially in socialist countries, the unemployed poor were put to work in paid jobs called "work relief." During the Great Depression, the federal government established the Works Progress Administration (WPA), which put the unemployed poor to work in a wide variety of jobs, e.g., building parks, roads and sewers and supplying aids to schools, hospitals, healthcare agencies and nonprofit social agencies. The program even included artists painting murals in public buildings and musicians putting on free concerts. Another method is called work for relief. This simply requires that the able-bodied recipients work without pay in exchange for benefits, as was done in workhouses and poor farms. This is done today in many places, in what is called "workfare," as mentioned previously, which expects recipients to report for work mostly for laboring jobs such as street and office cleaning. Such work is without pay but sometimes the recipients receive extra benefits. One problem with these programs is the extent to which they displace paid labor, though they are an effective way of dealing with aid to the unemployed, especially the longtime unemployed who have used up their unemployment benefits.

Delivery Systems of Social Welfare Programs

Along with means for providing social welfare programs are considerations of the level of service, funding, delivery, and relationships between public, nonprofit and commercial programs. In regard to levels of service, there is often a feeling that human services such as schools, hospitals, and social services ought to be provided by organizations operating on the local level where, in the spirit of togetherness, there can be more community involvement in the nature and quality of service provided. Often new and experimental services that states and the federal government are unwilling to try can be provided by localities. However, as states and municipalities vary greatly in their tax bases that affect funding to local services, there is general agreement that there must be considerable federal and state aid to localities according to the need. Conversely, it is felt that programs requiring large transfers of funds, such as social insurance benefits for retirement, unemployment, and health care, are best provided at the state and national level. This recognizes that the economy is increasingly national, with considerable mobility, and that justice requires all should get the same benefits and pay taxes according to their ability to pay regardless of where they live.

A national standard for human rights calls for all localities to meet basic human rights in the provision of services for nutrition, housing, economic security, education, healthcare and necessary social services. Conservatives who seek to avoid the redistribution of income to fund social welfare services want to limit what they have to pay in federal taxes on income and businesses; hence, they prefer that welfare services be provided by state and local governments receiving only federal block grants rather than federal aid for all eligible persons. Conversely, most state and local governments want substantial federal support for costly services such as healthcare, as they do not want to raise the taxes needed to fund these programs. If taxes in a given state become far higher than taxes in surrounding states, then the higher-tax states have a more difficult time attracting businesses.

Delivery-systems analysis increasingly involves considerations of the relationship between public and private social welfare services. Charitable activities by churches and private associations preceded the establishment of the public welfare state system. The latter developed as there was more recognition of human rights, including the rights to health and welfare services, which required more funding than could be provided by voluntary giving. That led to discussion of public and private relationships. One was the idea of complementary private services that exist parallel to public services with different functions. Social services such as childcare would be voluntarily funded and financial assistance would be provided by public agencies. The other concept was that of an "extension ladder," with private agencies providing services that go beyond those of public agencies, such as new and experimental programs.

Until recently, public and private services were mostly complementary. In nonprofit services, hospitals and physicians in private practice often provided healthcare at reduced rates, on the basis of the patient's ability to pay. In contrast, public health services were provided for the poor, primarily in public, general hospitals and outpatient clinics located in central cities. Public- hospital care was also provided by states and localities for special- needs populations, such as those with mental illness and tuberculosis. In the area of aid to the poor, those with temporary needs were helped by private charities, while those with longterm needs were cared for in public almshouses. The Great Depression revealed the inadequacy of private charities to meet financial needs, and led to the establishment of public welfare programs to provide public aid to low-income persons in their homes rather than in almshouses. There was also the significant development of public social insurance for the financial security of the retired, permanently handicapped and unemployed. The Depression also led to building public housing projects for the poor in slum-clearance efforts.

In recent years, the dividing line between private and public services has eroded, due primarily to the rising cost of healthcare, which made it more difficult for patients to pay what nonprofit health services and private physicians needed to charge to cover costs. This situation led to the utilization of third-party payments from private health insurance and from Medicare, Medicaid, and the children's health insurance program. The rising cost of healthcare increased the costs of private health insurance, creating the need for some public subsidies (Abramovitz, 1986). Hence, there is more use of public funds for the payment of services provided by private nonprofit and commercial services. All of this has the positive effect of not segregating poor and low-income persons into public facilities provided for them, which are often lower quality services that are overcrowded and understaffed. The purchase of care from nonprofit and commercial agencies enables low-income persons to receive more equal care alongside more affluent persons. The problem is that nonprofit services vary greatly in quality, according to the availability of private funding, and what they can charge patients who can afford to pay the full costs.

There are several concerns in using public funds to purchase services from private nonprofit and commercial organizations. The main one is what rate to pay and how to control costs. The rate paid affects the quality of services rendered, and public agencies have the obvious obligation of monitoring the quality of services rendered, including the number and quality of staff employed. In some cases, as with nursing homes, this may require negotiating individual rates based on costs, such as those needed to cover rent, mortgage payments, or new construction. Controlling costs often calls for control of what services are paid for, so that patients get the services they need but in the most effective and efficient way. Particularly in health and mental health services, public purchase of service and third-party payments by private and public health insurance call for the use of managed care service for determining what services are needed and for how long. This often requires prior approval of hospitalization and treatments to determine what services are needed, how much the patient can benefit and some approval as to the length of service (Sabin, 1997). Managed care services need to be as capable as possible and allow patients and clients to have some easily accessible means of appeal.

Other developments are public grants, contracts and subsidies to private agencies to provide needed services. This is being done increasingly in funding moderate- and low-income housing developments in place of grants to public housing authorities, and for poverty programs dealing with employments that include provision of childcare, transportation, and training programs. The advantage of doing this is that it facilitates the mixture of private funds, from gifts and foundations, with public funds to provide the service.

Another advantage is that it gets the support of private agencies and their constituencies behind the public funding. This is especially helpful in generating community support for the provision of low-income housing. Such housing often draws considerable local opposition by those who feel threatened by too many low-income families, who are perceived as composed of low-status minority groups that have a multitude of problems and are the source of much anti-social behavior.

However, there are negatives as well as positives to these arrangements. Conservatives generally prefer the contracting out to private and commercial operations in competitive bidding, which they argue lowers costs and makes for greater efficiency. The use of contracting is clearly helpful for highly specialized services such as special residential care, which would be costly for public agencies to duplicate. But on the negative side, private contracting is often a means to lower wages and break public employee unions. Such contracting can lead to a lot of buck-passing regarding responsibilities and, hence, the need for oversight as to contract compliance. Aid to private agencies is often justified as a means of getting around governmental regulations. The effect of this is mostly negative, such as avoiding civil service requirements, which can result in hiring persons based on favoritism, and avoiding fiscal accountability as to how public funds are actually spent. Efforts are sometimes made to encourage private agencies to take responsibility and pick up the "slack" when public agencies fail to provide needed services. For example, in Connecticut, private agencies were called to a meeting about the need to pick up on aid to those cut off from welfare. The outcome was, perhaps, fortunate, as the private agencies told the Connecticut welfare department the responsibility could not be passed off to them.

In this regard, it is important to remember that charity does not replace justice. Many conservatives who desire to avoid any redistribution of income want to make increased use of private, donated funds to provide limited services, often in the form of food and health services, in place of entitlement rights. Private donations to charities usually provide very limited help and a considerable portion of the giving may go to fundraising costs. Hence, a better use of donations may be to advocacy agencies, such as Bread for the World, which lobby for increased public funding for food and nutrition programs.

Private agencies are increasingly facing more difficulties in fundraising in the face of rising costs, and have had to seek more public grants, contracts and subsidies. This results in constraints as to what they can do and to greater instability, especially in relying on time-limited grants. As a result, many have had to close due to lost funding. The use of public funds for the provision of services by religious groups has the obvious advantage of gaining public acceptance, but often leads to the problem of restricting hiring to members of the denomination and forcing persons of other religions to use the service.

Taxes and the Struggle for Justice

The provision of public social welfare services depends on increasing taxes in order to pay for the benefits. Perhaps nowhere has the struggle for social justice been more bitterly fought than on who pays taxes for social welfare programs. Historically taxes have been seen as those levied by oppressive and colonial governments to finance their rule. The Bible is full of stories about paying taxes to the occupying Roman government. The American Revolution emphasized taxation without representation. This led to taxes being seen as the evil taking away of people's hard-earned money for the benefit of a repressive, social dominant force. To this day, this paradigm is used as the basis for not only opposing increasing taxes but advocating for their reduction. Over time, a new paradigm emerged, as concepts of democracy and social justice emerged. Governments came to be seen as more of a means for the provision of human services, especially health, education and welfare services, which raised the issue of who would pay taxes to support these services.

A major axiom of social justice that applies to human services is "from each according to his ability, to each according to his need." This makes the point that social justice deals with the redistribution of income to provide human services in the name of basic human rights and equality. In recent years, the class struggle—which is sometimes expressed as the "1 percent versus the 99 percent"—is most apparent in the struggle for and against proportional and progressive individual and corporation income taxes. One of the biggest victories for social justice was the passage of the federal income tax amendment in 1916, which taxed according to ability to pay and has become the main instrument for the funding of the welfare state. The capitalist market economy is regarded as leading to a great concentration of income that, in the name of social justice and equality, needs to be redistributed to middle and working class persons.

Another development in achieving greater equality was to deal with the concentration of wealth by enacting estate taxes on inherited wealth. Those opposed to income and inheritance taxes have argued that this deprives persons of income justly earned in the marketplace, destroys incentives to invest in order to increase income, and that these taxes reduce needed investment capital. Those supporting income taxes argue that there is little evidence of any correlation between taxes and incentives to invest or on the volume of investment, and thus the volume of investment depends on the existence of investment opportunities generated by increased consumer income that increases the demand for goods and services.

The proponents of social welfare and other public programs for education and infrastructure development such as highways and utilities point out that these tax-funded expenditures have a very positive effect on productivity and economic growth. Social insurance expenditures that go to all for retirement, disability, healthcare and unemployment, plus means-tested programs, provide income that increases the demand for goods and services, which keeps the economy functioning. Those who try to argue that social welfare expenditures are a drag on the economy seem mostly to imply that high taxes create an incentive to move production overseas, whereas clearly the main incentive for this is to lower labor costs.

Taxes can be classified as regressive, proportional, or progressive. Regressive taxes are those that tax lower incomes at a higher rate. Good examples of this are consumption taxes on sales and services and other consumer items such as gasoline, restaurant meals and hotel rooms. These taxes are seen as regressive because lower-income persons spend a larger percentage of their incomes on consumption items. Consumption taxes become less regressive if food and household items are excluded from sales taxes, as persons spend about the same for these regardless of income. Another example of regressive taxes are payroll taxes for the social insurances, such as Social Security and unemployment compensation, which do not include other sources of income, such as from investments. Proportional taxes tax incomes at about the same rate. There is some debate as to whether real estate taxes are proportional, on the basis that the wealthy live in more costly housing. Some say that this is less so as the wealthy are holding much less of their wealth in real estate. Others point out that large families need larger, more costly houses. Most income tax levies tend to be progressive and increase rates as income increases. Estate taxes on inherited wealth are progressive, in that only high-income persons pay.

As an indicator of how regressive, proportional, and progressive federal taxes are, the Congressional Budget Office regularly analyzes the effective taxes paid as a proportion of family income for each quintile of income distribution. The effective tax rate is a combination of four federal taxes: income tax, payroll tax, excise tax, and corporate income tax. Over twenty years, the effective tax rate has decreased, but is progressive over the quintiles including the top 5 percent, and has decreased more for the lower quintiles (See Table 4.1 on the next page).

The federal tax structure is moving more toward social justice objectives of being more progressive. Tax cuts (excluding the top 5 percent) would accomplish social justice objectives, and additionally may stimulate the economy and reduce the federal debt. The top 5 percent spend less income on consumer goods and services, so a tax cut for them would do little to stimulate economic demand. Further analysis of data not shown indicates that payroll taxes are proportional for the four lowest quintiles. That supports taking the cap off the payroll tax to make it proportional for all, which could help fund Social Security benefits. Data also indicates that the federal income tax is progressive and needs to be used for the redistribution of income through various social welfare programs, including the use of income tax credits.

State and local taxes tend to be more regressive. The state of Connecticut has one of the largest differences in income inequalities of any state (Hero, 2007). Noteworthy is that the Connecticut structure is regressive, with the effective rate decreasing from lowest to highest income and, compared to the federal effective taxes, is almost double for the bottom two quintiles (See Table 4.2 on the next page). It shows that for Connecticut, sales and excise taxes are regressive, that property taxes tend to be more proportional, and income taxes more progressive.

This indicates that states that make more use of income taxes and less of sales and excise taxes can have a more progressive tax system in accord with social justice objectives. As the effective rate is much lower for the top 5 percent of income earners, state income tax increases for this group should increase in order to balance state budgets.

Table 4.1

Total Effective Federal Tax Rate

Year	Lowest 20%	Second 20%	Middle 20%	Fourth 20%	Highest 20%	Top 10%	Top 5%	Top 1%
1980	7.7%	14.1%	18.7%	21.5%	27.3%	29.6%	31.8%	37.0%
1990	8.9%	14.6%	17.9%	20.6%	25.1%	26.1%	27.0%	28.8%
2000	6.4%	13.0%	16.6%	20.5%	28.0%	29.6%	31.0%	33.0%
2010	5.8%	12.3%	16.1%	20.5%	27.1%	28.5%	29.7%	31.2%

Source: Tax Policy Center, 2011; Congressional Budget Office, 2004

Table 4.2

Connecticut State and Local Taxes in 2007

Tax	Lowest 20%	Second 20%	Middle 20%	Fourth 20%	Highest 20%	Of the Top 20%, Next: 15%	4%	1%
Sales & Excise Taxes	6.3%	4.5%	3.5%	3.0%	27.3%	2.1%	1.3%	0.7%
Property Taxes	5.5%	3.9%	4.2%	4.5%	25.1%	3.9%	3.3%	0.9%
Income Taxes	0.1%	1.4%	2.9%	3.6%	28.0%	29.6%	4.0%	5.0%
Total Taxes	12.0%	9.9%	10.7%	11.0%	27.1%	10.2%	8.7%	6.5%

Source: Institute on Taxation and Economic Policy, 2009

With growing power, conservatives have been able to hold down increases in income, estate and real estate taxes, and get them reduced. In bringing this about they have resorted to several tactics. The main one is controlling public expenditures by calling for balanced budgets and a cap on expenditures that avoids pressures to increase taxes. Some states have put a cap on the increase of income and other taxes. An effort used mostly on the federal level has been to advocate income tax reductions primarily for the wealthy and businesses as a means of economic stimulus and as an instrument for economic growth. Success of this trickledown economics is highly questionable, and incomes have become more unequal as a result of income tax reductions for the wealthy. Those advocating tax cuts for the wealthy have attempted to sell these decreases by giving middle and lower income persons modest reductions. Some extremists advocate for abolishing income taxes and replacing them with some form of capitation tax that taxes all individuals equally regardless of income, such as an expanded consumption tax that would tax most persons relatively the same regardless of income. The result would be a total victory for the wealthy in the struggle between different socio-economic groups, as lower income persons would probably pay as much as a quarter of their income in taxes and the wealthy just one or 2 percent. This can be understood as expressing the justice of the market economy and the survival of the fittest ethos that results in great inequality of income. It is totally opposed to any idea of using social welfare payments as a means of redistributing income.

There have also been efforts to expand the use of regressive sales taxes by expanding coverage to more services and the use of "sin taxes" on such things as tobacco and alcohol. There have also been efforts to reduce real estate taxes. One argument, supported by many liberals, is a reduced real estate tax will produce more desirable economic growth by fostering more regional planning as municipalities will have less incentive to compete with each other for business and industrial locations in order to build up their tax bases. Others that oppose reductions of real estate taxes feel that they tend to be proportional to the extent that they levy more taxes on costly real estate used by businesses and industries and by high-income persons. They wonder how much individuals living in a house worth hundreds of thousands of dollars-making them among the wealthiest in the world-need tax relief. One concern is how much the loss of needed tax income from real estate taxes will be replaced and whether it will be replaced by greater use of regressive sales taxes or by more proportional and progressive income taxes.

President Franklin Roosevelt's advisor Harry Hopkins allegedly stated: "We will tax and tax, spend and spend, and elect and elect." This expressed the political success of taxing the wealthy, spending it for the welfare of the populace and getting their votes to win elections. This was an effective expression of populist politics based on the greater numbers of middle income and working class voters. In the years since the election of President Obama, the growing power of conservatives has greatly eroded this expression of populism so that legislatures with liberal majorities have trouble raising income taxes.

Much of the success in holding down taxes reflects a growing division among working class persons about social welfare expenditures that are seen as benefiting persons different from themselves such as those of different gender, racial and ethnic groups and those in different circumstances such as the aged and the unemployed. Thus the challenge involves forming coalitions along social class lines. This involves informing the public about the increasing unfairness of the tax system, especially with the growing gap in income between the wealthy and the rest, and the benefits derived from increased expenditures for human services. This in turn calls for developing more universal services that help more lower and middle class persons with rising costs of necessities such as medical care and housing not just aiding the poorest. Another program with a broad base of beneficiaries is the Earned Income Tax Credit (EITC) that supplements the income of a large number of low-income working persons.

One of the best ways to increase taxes is to tie the expansion of human service programs with tax sources needed to fund them.

This happens automatically in states and localities that are required to submit a balanced budget. What happens most often in local governments is that real estate taxes are increased in order to balance the budget.

Another method is to set up special funds for special purposes that are tied to a definite revenue source. The biggest example is the Social Security Trust fund that is tied to the payroll tax, and the Federal Highway Trust Fund tied to a federal gasoline tax. There are also housing funds tied to conveyance taxes on real estate transactions. Most of these employ some form of sales tax, a favorite one being a cigarette tax to fund special programs. Because of the regressive nature of sales and payroll taxes, this method of funding appeals to conservatives.

Strategies for increasing taxes on wealth involve pushing such things as a millionaires tax-higher income tax rates only for the very wealthy. In many places it should be possible to form a strong enough coalition to roll back cuts made in federal and state income taxes on the wealthy in order to pay for universal medical care and housing subsidies. Many, including some wealthy, support the need for estate taxes as the concentration of wealth is seen as undesirable and against social justice. There are many other approaches, including increasing the short term capital gains tax on those who made large speculative profits on the sale of property and other investments, and who have done nothing to improve the property or increase the value of their investments. Many agree that speculative investment tends to create boom and bust situations that destabilize the economy of which the stock market crash of 1929 is a vivid example. In this connection, one can remember receiving a report that indicated the value of ones investments had increased by $30,000 over a three month period without any action and saying to ones self, what have I done to deserve this? Of course one would ask this all the more if he lost this amount.

Much can be done to close tax loopholes that appear unjustified. One obvious one would be taking the cap off the payroll tax for Social Security. There are many loopholes in corporation taxes that were passed due to lobbyists working with certain legislators. There may be many instances where the political situation has changed so that with a little effort they can be repealed. As has been stated, a basic ethos of social justice is "from each according to his ability to each according to his need" that calls for at least a proportional if not progressive tax system.

There are a lot of those who are compassionate about the needs of others, but strongly opposed to paying a just proportion of their income and wealth toward meeting those needs. Such persons seem as greedy hypocrites. In the parable of the Good Samaritan, they can be seen as those who passed by without aiding to the best of their ability the man who had been attacked by thieves. The parable makes the point that the Good Samaritan did not just take the man and dump him on the care of the innkeeper but in accordance with his ability left money to care for his keep. This is especially revealed when church groups deal with social justice concerns. An example is a resolution introduced at a church convention calling for a proportional or progressive tax system based on ability to pay. It was pointed out that there were numerous passages in the Bible calling for sharing one's abundance, and that taxes were a means of sharing. This advocacy of progressive taxes flushed out the conservatives who called it communistic and succeeded in voting it down, highlighting the need to push as an essential ethos of social justice the sharing of a just portion of one's wealth and income with others through the payment of taxes as a social obligation. In this connection one would like to see a reenactment of Dickens "A Christmas Carol" in which a person called Scrooge would oppose sharing his wealth to pay taxes for universal medical care and after seeing the need of the Tiny Tims who do not have health insurance and seeing himself as a greedy unloved person, would be converted to advocate for an income tax increase to pay for universal medical care.

Fiscal Welfare

The late British writer Richard Titmuss (1958) referred to three forms of welfare: social welfare, fiscal welfare provided through the tax system, and occupational welfare provided by employers as employee benefits. Fiscal welfare deals with the provision of benefits by tax relief, largely in the form of income tax deductions, tax credits, and tax exemptions that reduce the amount of taxes paid. Income tax deductions in effect lower the cost of certain expenditures and have the effect of providing a price discount. As they reduce the amount of tax liability, they benefit most those who are in the high income tax brackets. Income tax credits reduce the amount of the final tax bill and have the effect of providing financial aid as they reduce tax obligations. They provide more help for low-income persons for whom the tax credit is a greater portion of their income tax, and serve as a form of income redistribution. Tax credits can be refundable for those whose tax credit is more than their tax obligations, and hence are a means of aiding very low-income persons. Some extreme conservatives oppose the provision of a refundable credit, as they want the credit limited to tax relief. This clearly places them in the ranks of the oppressors of the poor.

Tax exemptions are given in the form of real estate tax exemptions to nonprofit charitable and religious organizations, and to public and low-income housing projects. For individuals, tax exemptions are applied to a portion of income that is diverted to savings accounts for retirement, health care, and as a means of providing savings for low-income persons to use as a down payment on a home or for a small business investment.

Fiscal welfare applies to both corporations and individuals. Corporate tax relief is provided for such things as venture capital investments and for capital expenditures to increase productivity and is clearly justified to the extent that it increases economic growth and improves the standard of living and economic security of all. Corporate tax deductions are also used for fostering employee benefits such as health insurance contributions. They aid private welfare programs through corporate tax deductions for such things as contributions to welfare programs provided by nonprofit organizations. Tax deductions for individuals have the effect of lowering the costs of needed expenditures such as mortgage tax deductions that lower the costs of homeownership and deductions for childcare and health care. Deductions for real estate and other taxes have the advantage of easing their cost and hence make them more acceptable.

Fiscal welfare is popular with conservatives who pay a lot of taxes and like tax relief. Fiscal welfare is an easy and often sought out means for effecting social policies in a market economy by providing deductions for desirable expenditures such as energy saving devices and for medical and child care costs. Providers of these services such as banks and realtors also support fiscal welfare for mortgage interest deductions. In the legislative process, tax deductions avoid having to deal with the appropriations process and the need to balance expenditures with tax revenue. However, some economists like to refer to tax relief as tax expenditures, as it means that fewer taxes are collected and therefore less revenue is available for needed public programs (Anderson, 2010; New, 2009). Recently critics have referred to tax relief for the wealthy as reverse Robin Hood, when tax relief is financed through cutting programs for the poor or increasing taxes for middle and low-income earners (Herbert, 2003; Rietmulder, 2011; Wayne, 2002).

When viewed as tax expenditures this raises the question, who really pays? To the extent that lost revenue is supplemented by increasing taxes, the question is what taxes? Usually when tax expenditures result in less real estate tax revenue, most feel that tax expenditures cause increased real estate taxes for the rest. It is less certain that the loss of income tax revenue is made up by other increases in income taxes due to strong opposition from conservatives. Most likely it results in reducing expenses through program cuts where one of the victims is likely to be social welfare programs for the poor that are opposed by conservatives. Also when viewed as tax expenditures, it points to the need to evaluate them, as is done for other expenditures, for their cost effectiveness and what they accomplish in achieving social justice objectives. There are questions as to how effective and efficient tax reductions are in accomplishing these objectives and whether they are mainly just a means of providing tax relief. The problem is that many deductions are for things that persons and businesses have the income to do anyway, and those with low income do not benefit. For example, income tax deductions for mortgage payments provide more relief to the wealthy who own an expensive home and do little for low-income persons who do not qualify for a mortgage. Also many employers that have capital intensive operations and pay high wages can easily pay for basic health insurance costs without tax deductions, but labor intensive low wage employment, for which the health insurance costs are just as high, cannot afford to pay for these costs even with deductions. Increasingly employers are dropping their coverage (Appleby, 2007).

In economic development many companies would invest in new machinery without deductions, whereas other new and smaller companies cannot afford the equipment even with deductions. Many businesses get property tax relief for locating in a community where they would probably locate anyway because there is strong demand for their products and services. This indicates that a more efficient use of tax dollars is to limit tax expenditures for such things as income tax deductions for mortgage payments and apply the increased tax revenue to the provision of low and moderate income housing, which would serve more social justice purposes. Also many new and small businesses need aid in the form of grants and subsidies, not just tax relief in order to grow. Thus tax relief also does not replace the need for various forms of social welfare benefits to meet the needs of low-income persons. Tax relief does not eliminate the need for grants and subsidies and other means to lower costs to private organizations to provide employee benefits and make investments for desirable economic growth.

These considerations can also apply to efforts of the investment banking industry to increase business by securing income tax exemptions for payments to personal savings accounts, retirement, and health care, and for low-income persons to save for a college education, down payment on a home, and owning a small business. The problem is that most higher income persons save for these purposes whereas many low-income persons would not be able to save enough even with exemptions for it to be of any real benefit and would need far more help for retirement, health insurance, a college education, homeownership or to start a small business.

The lack of savings also can be another way to blame the victims of poverty. It implies a special virtue in being frugal and ignores the fact that everyone has his or her own lifestyle and needs that determine how one spends money. It also ignores the fact that the more income one has the easier it is to take care of lifestyle needs and have money left over for savings. It should be clear that very low-income persons struggle to meet basic needs for which they need help, and cannot afford to save. There is also the question of giving tax relief only for savings accounts that are managed by investment banks for a fee that seems to be primarily a form of subsidizing investment banks. Also it should be clear that a savings account does not substitute for insurance protection against risks such as health care needs and death. Low-income persons need protection from accumulating large debts and paying high interest charges that lowers their standard of living.

Tax Credit Programs

An income tax deduction provides the most tax relief for high-income persons, who are in high income tax brackets. Social justice objectives are better served by giving tax credits against tax owed, which provide greater relief to middle- and low- income persons.

For example, a universal child tax credit of a $1,000 per child is a much higher proportion of a low-income person's tax bill. Tax credit programs also have the advantage of being legislated as a part of the tax code, which can be adjusted to make up for the loss of tax revenue.

The tax credit method of financing social welfare benefits has appeal because of its association with tax reduction that is popular with laissez-faire conservatives. It largely helps the needy instead of those with high incomes and is provided as an entitlement to all eligible persons. It serves even more as an instrument for redistribution if those whose credit exceeds their tax liability are given a benefit in the form of a refund. The use of tax credits led to the popular federal Earned Income Tax Credit (EITC) program that provides tax credits to supplement earnings of low-income persons and has an appeal to employers as it relieves pressures to pay a living wage.

The EITC gives a low-income working person an income tax credit to supplement wages earned up to a certain level of income after which the credit is gradually reduced (United States Department of Treasury, 2011). It is especially designed to help low-income families by providing larger credits for families with one, two, or three children. In the 2011 tax year, the credit will increase to a plateau of $13,660 to $18,740 of taxable income, after which it is reduced up to a taxable income of $49,078 for a family with three or more children, beyond which no credit is given. The maximum tax credit payment for a family with three or more qualifying children will be $5,751 so that when reaching the plateau the family could be assured of a minimum annual income of $19,411, which is about what someone with a minimum wage of $10.11 an hour would earn (Internal Revenue Service, 2011). Thus, it is a means of supplementing the income of the increasing number of workers who for various reasons are required to work less than full time. EITC is supplemented by many states that provide an average of approximately 20 percent of the federal benefit.

EITC has proven an effective tool for eliminating poverty of the working poor, making work pay, and reducing income inequality. Roughly one in six of all families that file a federal income tax return receive an EITC benefit. Each year it lifts more than four million people out of poverty and takes more children out of poverty than any other federal program. The program was expanded during the Clinton administration. There are a number of proposals for its improvement. One would be to provide increased benefits for families with more than three children and to increase the benefit for single persons. The level of benefits should be increased so that all beneficiaries receive a minimum of least 125 percent of poverty so as to give all working poor the right to a decent income.

The federal child tax credit (CTC) gives an income tax credit of $1,000 per child to all families with dependent children, whose earned income is least $3,000 in 2011. This tax credit has the potential to benefit all, but poor households caring for children who earn less than $10,000 annually will not receive the full credit. Congress passed the Tax Relief Act of 2010, which extended the $3,000 CTC threshold until 2012. CTC can be further improved to include all low-income children and families by making it fully refundable and lowering the minimum income threshold to zero (RESULTS, 2011).

There are a number of other ways that tax credits could be used. One is to use them as part of a universal health insurance system by giving universal tax credits for part of the cost of private health insurance. Tax credits might also replace income exclusions for such things as retirement savings accounts that would provide more benefit for low-income persons. The obvious limit is that extensive tax credits would greatly reduce tax revenue needed for other purposes. Hence, there would have to be some increases in income tax rates so that higher income persons would pay more in increased taxes and make the system more redistributive. The amount of such a tax credit could be negotiated in tax legislation to increase income taxes for higher income persons to make up for the income that would be lost to finance the credit.

Occupational Welfare

Occupational welfare deals with employee benefits such as retirement pensions, and payment of medical, disability, and worker's compensation insurance. They are increasingly a vital means of providing economic and social security, particularly with the increasing cost of health care and the need to provide for more lengthy retirements due to increasing longevity. Some European nations require employers to provide these benefits in place of public programs, whereas other nations, particularly in health care, provide this solely through public programs. The advantage of requiring employers to provide benefits is that it avoids raising taxes. The disadvantage is that employers vary greatly in their ability to provide benefits.

One factor is size of the business, where the claims of a few employees at one time may cause a great financial strain for small businesses. This can be eased by enabling small businesses to join bigger plans at reduced cost. However, a bigger problem is the difference in employee benefit costs between capital intensive employments that have a few high paid employees, and labor intensive employments that need a large low paid labor force. An example is chemical companies and oil refiners that are capital intensive and need very little labor so that employee benefit costs are not a major factor; whereas the hospitality industry, hotels and restaurants, and the soft goods industry need a lot of low wage labor, so that employee benefits greatly increase labor costs. This is particularly true in the case of health insurance that costs the same for a low-wage and high-wage employee. Some would advocate for requiring all employers to provide benefits. This would increase the cost of products and services of labor-intensive businesses and may result in less demand for those products and services. For many economists these price increases would be the market economy working as it should in the allocation of goods and services according the costs of supply.

Most employee benefits have an insurance feature that involves the sharing of risks such as health and the length of life. Hence what is needed in health and retirement insurance is having a large pool of participants through group coverage that generally can provide more protection than individuals can get from purchasing their own health insurance and retirement plans. In the U.S. there is a mixture of employee benefits, individual benefits and public programs that creates a confusing challenge as to what is the best fit.

Retirement benefits historically have been provided by employer retirement pension plans that build on Social Security benefits and provide a defined fixed benefit as long as a person lives. Benefits are generally provided as a percentage of one's final pay that increases according to the length of time one has been participating in the plan. Small businesses can often join a larger retirement plan offered by business and professional associations such as chambers of commerce. Employers make regular contributions into a retirement fund for each covered employee. Most employers pay most of the contribution with each employee paying less. Employees are expected to contribute substantially more if spouses are added. Most agree that the defined benefit system has worked well in providing retirement security as one gets a fixed benefit for life. Many advocates of social justice believe ideally the benefit when combined with Social Security should replace about two-thirds of previous earnings. There is concern for employments that do not provide this security, so that their retirees have to rely solely on Social Security benefits that only provide basic security. One social justice concern are cases where employers offer much better retirement benefits for salaried executive staff than for the hourly workers.

There has been a recent trend away from defined benefit retirement pension plans. The main reason for the shift is that defined benefit plans have been subject to more government regulations that seek to protect the solvency of retirement funds by regulating the size of reserves and how they are invested. This has increased the cost of the plans for many businesses. Another factor in the shift has been the downsizing of many businesses due in part to the out sourcing of operations, so that there are fewer contributors into the retirement fund to help pay promised benefits. Another factor is also the difficulty in shifting retirement coverage when one changes employment or when companies are bought out by others with different plans.

The result is that many employers are shifting to provide individual retirement savings accounts that employees can draw out upon retirement as they see fit, but do not provide a lifelong defined benefit. Some individual plans are sponsored by employers, usually as a replacement for defined benefit plans previously offered. The employers manage these plans and most continue to pay at least half of the contributions. Another form of retirement savings accounts are called Individual Retirement Accounts (IRAs) which are purchased by individuals from investment brokers and insurance companies where the employee pays most of the management fees. Employers may make contributions to IRAs that are generally less than the ones they sponsor. Many employees use an IRA as a way to add onto their retirement savings over what they get from employment benefit plans and hence, strictly speaking, IRAs are not employee benefits. However, all employee contributions to individual savings accounts, both employers' sponsored and those bought by individuals, are entitled to have a part of their contributions excluded from their federal income tax. That makes them a part of fiscal welfare.

These individual retirement savings accounts provide less security in that the accumulated savings depend on how well their funds were invested. There is always the danger that years of accumulated savings may be severely reduced by a downturn in the value of the investments due mainly to a decline in the stock market. This happened for many plans in the 2008 recession. Many investment advisors believe as funds accumulate they should be moved to more fixed income investments such as bonds. This slows growth but provides protection against decline in the value of variable income assets such as stocks. Individuals can purchase defined benefit plans offered in the market by investment brokers and insurance companies, but requirements about the size of the reserves and how they are invested increase the costs so they cannot provide promised fixed benefits comparable to what most can save in a retirement savings account. This is countered somewhat by the fact that defined benefits are based on how long the employee has participated in the plan and hence many long time employees can receive larger defined benefits than they could receive from a less costly individual savings account. Hence one challenge is, what can be done to preserve defined benefit pension plans that provide greater lifetime security? That might call for some form of government aid such as giving more tax relief or some form of subsidy. Another possibility is to let employees join retirement plans offered by other employers, including government plans. Still another possibility is to enable employees who choose to do so to buy into an extension of their Social Security benefits to which employers would add increased payroll deductions. There needs to be exploration of whether this would provide greater protection at less cost to the employee than individual plans. This would also have the advantage of providing protection when one changes employment.

Another consideration, in the interest of social justice, is whether to require all employers to contribute a portion of their employees' wages into a plan that each employee might select. This could include defined benefit plans, individual savings plans that employers would provide or to IRAs. Such a requirement would make employee retirement benefits universal and provide protection for all. This would also address the problem that many employers would like to provide retirement benefits, but feel they cannot afford to do so unless their competitors do likewise. Providing retirement benefits for all in addition to Social Security should provide a real stimulus to the economy as it would increase consumer spending by retirees.

Employee Health Benefits

Many employers provide health benefits by contracting with a private health insurance company to manage the plan. Often large employers give employees a choice of several insurance plans they may join. Many companies in addition to basic health coverage provide benefits for dental care, drugs and medigap insurance for retirees receiving Medicare benefits and hence cover virtually all of the health expenses of employees and retirees. Some offer plans that for somewhat less cost provide for joining health maintenance plans and preferred provider plans where there is less choice of physicians. Most employers pay about 75 or 80 percent of the health insurance costs but usually expect employees to pay a much larger amount for inclusion of family coverage. Employers can deduct much of their expenditures from their federal and state income taxes.

Providing employee health benefits increasingly presents a problem for employers due to rising health care costs. This is particularly burdensome for low-wage and labor intensive employments and for small businesses. Consequently employers are drastically reducing benefits, increasing co-pays, or dropping coverage all together for new employees. Many employers are increasingly contracting work to private contractors who do not provide health insurance, or employ part-time workers who receive no employee benefits. Thus a major national problem is the growing number of persons who do not have health insurance coverage.

The federal health care reform act, entitled Patient Protection and Affordable Care Act (ACA), passed in March 2010. ACA was intended to move the U.S. toward universal health care and reduce the number of uninsured by an estimated 43 million. In regard to occupational welfare, it established many requirements for employer offered health insurance. The ACA requires that employees cannot be denied coverage for pre-existing conditions, employers must provide coverage for dependent children to continue their benefits up to age 26, and employers may not limit lifetime benefits paid.

Related to the provision of employee benefits for medical care is the provision of paid sick leave. There have been provisions in federal policies that employers provide sick leave that also includes the need to be home for the care of sick children. Most employers offer paid sick leave, but many especially small businesses, do not. Most have a cap on the accumulation of unused sick leave days, and that includes the need to be home to care for sick children. Advocates for paid sick days argue that sick employees should stay at home and not risk infecting others. In 2011, Connecticut became the first state to require certain employers to provide a minimum amount of paid sick leave. An alternative to requiring employers to offer paid sick days is to expand unemployment insurance to include paid sick leave benefits after a waiting period. It seems most employers could afford to provide one or two weeks of paid sick leave annually. The high cost of medical care makes illness a burden for families that also cannot afford the loss of pay. This is especially a problem for low-income families that do not have employer health benefits.

Another needed employee benefit is disability insurance. Individual employee savings accounts may work for retirement, but not so well for disability protection. For example if an employee is disabled at any early age, disability insurance would be badly needed, especially if the employee has not have accumulated enough savings for any real protection. Some employers provide disability insurance through group insurance that lowers the cost of premiums. For those employments that do not provide this coverage, employees only have disability insurance through Social Security. There needs to be means to make it easier for employers to provide disability coverage through tax credits or subsidies. If employees were given the option of buying into increased Social Security benefits this could also include disability benefits that are currently provided as a part of Social Security. There should also be a consideration to help employers provide long-term care insurance for employees. Employee benefits include worker's compensation for injuries incurred on the job, and occupational health and safety requirements imposed on employers by federal and state governments.

Social Welfare Programs Dealing with Unemployment

Economists have developed various classifications of unemployment according to the factors involved. The most basic is demand deficient unemployment that results when there is not enough aggregate demand for goods and services to employ all those in the labor market seeking employment. As was discussed above, this requires the use of the political economy to develop various job creating devices. The main ones include the increase of public expenditure to create jobs or the reduction of taxes on consumers so they have more to spend. Another job creation device include increases investments by lowering interest rates, providing more credit and providing tax incentives to increase productivity.

Second form of unemployment has been termed technological unemployment that comes about when employees are replaced by automation and other labor saving devices. This can be dealt with if technological unemployment increases productivity that can be used to increases the wages of the remaining employees without increasing prices. These higher wages are then spent on more goods and services that stimulates the economy and employs more people. As macro-economic analysis teaches, there can be as much unemployment in a low-wage labor-intensive economy as in a capital intensive high wage economy because low wage earners have little money to spend.

Related to this is what is a third form of unemployment, which is termed structural unemployment due to a mismatch between available skills and the demands of the labor market and between location of jobs and the location of available labor. Poverty programs with an emphasis on education and training seem largely based on the belief that unemployment is due to skill shortages. Some analysts pointed out that to prove that a training program resulted in increased employment, it is necessary to prove that jobs would not otherwise have been filled and employees were hired as a result of training received. In this regard there should be a distinction between those jobs that require a skill that can only be acquired by prolonged education, and training programs mostly provided at the technical school, college or university level, and those where the skill level is more relative than absolute and which can be filled by on-the job training.

In the latter it has been pointed out that many would be hired in an expanding labor market regardless of training. Further, the complaint of employers that they cannot fill jobs often means they cannot find employees with the skill levels they want at the wages they are willing to pay. It must be remembered that when skill levels are relative rather than absolute it is a matter of how far employers will have to reach down in skill levels in order to fill the job, and this depends on how tight the labor market is. Dealing with the structure of unemployment calls for identifying where there are labor shortages that require definite professional or prolonged job training.

In the current economy, this largely calls for recruiting and educating more engineers, scientists, nurses, other medical arts specialists, and those with skills in data processing, accounting and financial services among others. Skills in these areas are needed for developing new and better products and increased labor productivity and are essential for economic growth. There are clearly benefits to economic growth by increasing the education and general skill level of all those in the labor market, but the challenge is to identify and respond to where this is most needed. Greater educational attainment will not per-se lead to full employment and can just as well lead to better educated unemployed and those with low paying and part-time jobs. Thus there need to be public policies that will provide needed education and training opportunities at affordable costs and aid to students for living expenses.

A final form of unemployment is frictional unemployment the time between leaving one job and finding another one. It is here where unemployment insurance and termination benefits are most useful as they enable one to take time to explore what job opportunities there are or to recognize that they need retraining or to relocate. As jobs become more specialized it will be increasingly more important to have programs for job search, retraining and relocation assistance.

One consideration in dealing with unemployment is the size of the labor force, as unemployment is measured as a percentage of those in the labor force who are seeking employment. Hence, one way to deal with unemployment is to control who is in the labor force. One way to decrease the size of the labor market is to increase the number who are in full-time education and training programs. One reason for establishing a system of retirement benefits under Social Security was to take retirees out of the labor force and hence decrease the percentage of unemployed.

The size of the labor force is also the dominant factor in the debate over immigration policies. Most nations have immigration quotas that are geared to the needs of the labor market, as they do not want to flood it with an increased supply of low-paid workers who lower the level of wages, displace others and increase the rate of unemployment. Employers often oppose immigration restrictions so as to expand the pool of low-paid labor they can hire to keep their labor costs down. Many countries import temporary workers to harvest crops and for temporary economic development projects, and expect them to return home once the jobs are completed. The problem of importing foreign labor is further complicated when these laborers are comprised largely of certain racial and ethnic groups. This can create racial and ethnic tensions, and can hamper the struggle for social justice.

Another consideration in dealing with the size of the labor force is how many are involuntarily unemployed but have given up looking for a job because they think there is little chance of getting hired. It is hard to measure how many of these there are. It is estimated that if the unemployment rate included those who stopped looking for work and the underemployed, the rate of unemployment would almost double (Engel, 2010).

Since 1950 unemployment has fluctuated with the economy, indicating the main cause of unemployment is demand deficiency. From 1950 to 1974 the rate of unemployment generally ranged from a low of 2.9 percent in1953 to a high of 6.0 in 1971. During the recession of the mid '70s, unemployment rose to 8.5 percent in 1975 and stayed around 7 percent until 1986. Since 1992, unemployment had been falling, and in 2000 unemployment was at a three-decade low of 4 percent. However, in 2000 unemployment then saw a steady rise, as economic growth slowed, and the U.S. headed into a recession. In January 2011 the U.S. unemployment rate was at 9 percent (U.S. Bureau of Labor Statistics, 2011b). The rate has been substantially higher for those between the age of 16 and 25. Since 1950 it has been marked by a growing equality in wages between men and women. The unemployment rate for African Americans has been generally twice that of whites (U.S. Bureau of Labor Statistics, 2011c).

Programs for the Unemployed

Obviously it would be impossible to have a society, especially a capitalist one, in which everyone who wanted a job would get one. Also most agree there needs to be some level of unemployment to make it easier to fill jobs and allow for some selection. Also workers should be able to take some time to find the job they want. It should be noted that one way to reduce unemployment is to take persons such as children, the aged, blind, sick, disabled, and those needed in the home for child care, out of the labor market by social welfare programs that provide them and their families with needed income.

Article 25 of the Universal Declaration of Human Rights states that persons have the right to economic security in the event of unemployment. It is important to reiterate the problems that have to be faced in providing employment. One has been to emphasize equality of opportunity to compete for scarce jobs that only intensifies the competition and does little to increase overall employment and nothing to provide economic security for the unemployed. Policies dealing with equality of opportunity generally focus on improving the attributes of the unemployed, especially the level of education and job skills so they can better compete. As has been pointed out this will do little to increase overall employment and will only result in better educated unemployed and persons in low paying jobs. The other problem that has been highlighted is that aid for the able-bodied unemployed affects the justice of the labor market as it provides income that is not earned in exchange for labor. Historically this has resulted in meager, punitive and oppressive welfare programs for the unemployed that has included the use of workhouses, poor farms and auctioning off the poor to the lowest bidder who was to get as much work out of them as possible in exchange for their keep. In the U.S., welfare aid for the able-bodied unemployed has remained a part of what is called the general assistance program provided by local and state governments-that is what remains of the Poor Law-without the federal aided programs of aid to dependent children the aged, blind, and disabled. The aid provided remains meager, punitive and oppressive.

Partly a result of the backlash against the civil rights movement and the growing power of the conservatives, many states and localities cut off the able-bodied unemployed aid entirely and time limits were imposed on federal and state programs of aid to able-bodied mothers with dependent children. These cuts have mainly hurt unemployed African Americans, whose unemployment rates double that of whites. There is little evidence that the cut offs forced mothers into jobs that would not otherwise have been filled. If these cuts did anything it made it easier to fill part-time jobs without employee benefits, and that removed few from poverty.

The most successful and accepted approach to providing economic security for the unemployed have been unemployment insurance programs. Unemployment insurance programs pay benefits to workers whose employment was terminated, regardless of what other source of income they have and hence, does not qualify as a welfare program for the unemployed poor. Unemployment insurance focuses on the functioning of the economy, not the attributes of the victims. In this regard one of the most commonly used statistics in dealing with the functioning of the economy is how many persons have applied for unemployment benefits. It is generally agreed that paying benefits to the unemployed is one of the best ways to stimulate the economy as it counters the downward spiral of unemployment causing less consumer spending and hence more unemployment. Further, this gets around the problem of receiving a benefit that is not earned as it is funded mostly by a tax on payrolls on employee earnings that is placed in a fund out of which benefits are paid.

In the U.S. unemployment compensation is provided by a federal-state program that is a part of the Social Security Act of 1935. Using the taxing power of the federal government, the Act levies a payroll tax of 3% on payrolls; 2.7% is forgiven if the states levy a tax to fund their own systems. Eligibility is fairly uniform among states. Generally employees are required to work in covered employment for half of the year preceding unemployment and after a waiting period of one or two weeks are entitled to benefits for six months. In times of high unemployment this may be extended by 13 weeks and in times of unusually high unemployment even further that is federally funded. Benefits are paid weekly and generally replace about half of previous wages with a ceiling as to the maximum benefit. The waiting period is lengthened if the worker voluntarily quits or is engaged in a labor dispute. Only a few states provide extra benefits for dependents. Covered employment usually excludes farm labor, part-time labor and small businesses. In 2009, due to limitations in coverage and to benefit limits, less than half of the unemployed received benefits (Hagenbaugh, 2009).

The unemployed who are not receiving unemployment benefits must seek help from state and local general assistance programs that, especially in conservative times, result in policies that blame the victim, and are punitive and oppressive. Thus one of the big challenges in the quest for social justice is how to provide economic security for the able-bodied unemployed who are not receiving unemployment benefits (Shapiro, 1992). This could be done by shortening the time one has to be employed to be eligible, and lengthen the time one can draw benefits. Ideally benefits should replace two-thirds of previous earnings and provide for the number of dependents. For those who have exhausted their benefits there needs to be consideration of a federal-state means-tested program of benefits. This would be similar to the federal supplementary social insurance (SSI) program provided to the aged, blind and disabled that supplements Social Security benefits. State labor departments that also administer unemployment, insurance rather than welfare departments, would administer the federal-state means-tested program. As it deals with those who have been laid off due to downsizing, outsourcing and other economic factors, the focus would be on the functioning of the economy and the labor market and away from the blaming the victim approach of welfare programs. It would be especially helpful to economically depressed areas faced with long time unemployment and would serve as an economic stimulus. The program could also accept referrals of able-bodied employable recipients from general assistance and Temporary Assistance for Needy Families (TANF) that would get them away from welfare department programs.

The program could deal with the problem of the long term unemployed receiving benefits that are not earned, by making extensive use of programs that put them to work. There are two ways to do this. One is called work relief that provides paying jobs for the eligible poor unemployed. The other called "work for relief" or "workfare" does not pay wages but requires recipients to work in exchange for their welfare benefits, though some may get a grant increase for working. Many nations, especially socialist ones, have labor market programs and provide wage subsidies to put most of the long-term unemployed to work with some limiting it to just the unemployed poor (Human Resources and Skills Development Canada, 1994).

During the Great Depression there was substantial use of work relief in the federal Works Progress Administration program. This provided jobs in government projects, including work in parks and conservation projects. Others were employed as helpers in schools and other public and nonprofit agencies. It even involved employing musicians and actors to put on public performances and artists to paint murals. The idea was to provide extra add on jobs rather than displace those in permanent jobs. Under the fiscal year 2010 reauthorization of the Temporary Assistance for Needy Families (TANF) program, states have been under pressure to put at least half of their able-bodied recipients to work. Many prefer to use "work for relief" in which recipients work for their benefit and not for pay as this costs less and there is more incentive to look for paying jobs.

Of special concern is the unemployment of youths finishing their education and entering the labor force. Almost everywhere this group has the highest rate of unemployment among the able-bodied. Youth who are socially disconnected due to lack of social supports, poverty, and racial discrimination become more disconnected when they are unemployed. Often these youths drop out from making a social contribution and cause other social problems. As more is learned about neuroscience, it is revealed that the brain is not fully developed until the early twenties, which may lead to problems in judgment and behavior. Clearly these youths need the stability and control that come from employment. Hence most nations have felt the need to establish special programs for youth employment or that provide further education.

Some of these programs have taken on a military model or Job Corps that provides for living and working together. In January, 2011 the U.S. Bureau of Labor Statistics (2011c) reported that 40.9 percent of Americans 16 to 24 were unemployed. In much of the U.S. the problem of unemployed youth has been made worse by cutting them off public assistance and cutting youth employment programs. What is needed is to develop a federal-state program that provides employment and/or education and training programs for all eligible unemployed youth under the age of twenty-five. In order to provide the right to economic security this should be an entitlement program that puts all eligible unemployed youth that lack income for basic sustenance to work in work relief programs. These programs could consist of public service jobs in public and nonprofit agencies doing such things as help with childcare, transportation, road maintenance, and conservation projects. Those not put to work should be provided with enough income for basic sustenance. Those who could benefit from it should be helped to attend further education and job training programs with an allowance for the program costs and an entitlement to sufficient income for basic needs. This should include a provision for health care, as too many youths do not have health insurance. In the developmental process, adolescence and young adulthood is a time when health and mental health conditions arise. Especially in mental health the developmental stage of adolescence is associated with the onset of depression, schizophrenia, addictions and borderline personality disorders. These cases need to be treated in the mental health system, and not the criminal justice system (as is too often the case). Also too many youth cannot afford rent. They become homeless and are badly in need of rental assistance benefits. Opportunities for youth to join public service programs such as the Peace Corps and job corps helps reduce unemployment and should be expanded, but those programs do not replace the need to provide economic security for all unemployed youths as an entitlement.

Economic Security Through Social Insurance

In addition to the federal-state program of unemployment insurance, the other social insurance program provided under the Social Security Act of 1935 was the Old Age, Survivors and Disability Insurance program (OASDI) that provides benefits to those in covered employment for retirees and their spouses, for surviving widows with minor children, and for those permanently and totally disabled. Benefits are financed by payroll tax of 12.5 percent paid half by employees and half by employers that is then placed into the Social Security Trust Fund. There is an income limit on the payroll tax that is adjusted periodically to deal with the increase in wage level. The 2011 limit is $106,800-this remains at the 2009 base level due to no cost-of-living adjustment (Social Security Administration, 2010). This was included to deal with the fact that there was an upper limit on benefits. Retirement benefits pay a fixed monthly benefit for as long as one lives based on approximately 40 percent of previous earnings with a larger percentage being provided to lower income persons, making Social Security redistributive. Previous earnings on which the level of benefits is determined are adjusted to reflect changes in the level of wages and the benefits paid are adjusted annually to the cost of living. The program is also redistributive in that benefits are paid to widows and spouses including divorced spouses where the marriage lasted at least 10 years.

There are also disability benefits paid to persons with serious physical and mental handicaps that prevent them from working. Disability benefits have been a major factor in providing for community care for mentally handicapped individuals. Disabilities are expected to last a year or until death, but benefits will continue as long as the condition lasts. Benefits are considered the same as retirement and survivors benefits as spouses and dependent children are eligible as long as the employee worked in covered employment for at least half time from ages twenty-four to thirty-one. Past age thirty-one an employee must have worked for half time in the last10years preceding eligibility. Funds from the payroll tax are placed in a special disability trust fund out of which benefits are paid. In order to control costs, persons applying for benefits must submit to a rigorous examination of their condition. There are concerns that eligibility needs to be relaxed for those who are physically able to work, but because of age are not likely to find employment.

There are ways in which Social Security could be improved. One problem is that widows can now elect to receive a widow's benefit that is roughly half of the spouse's benefit or receive their own benefit (whichever is higher), but not both. With more and more women working, most receive a larger benefit on their own. Those receiving widows' benefits receive the spouse's benefit when he dies, but for couples living on two benefits, the death of the spouse cuts the income almost in half as the surviving spouse cannot receive both benefits. Hence there might be consideration of allowing couples to receive a reduced combined benefit that would continue in the event of the death of a spouse.

The Social Security program (OASDI) has been highly successful in providing basic economic security for the aged. In 1958 one third of those over age 65 were living in poverty, whereas by 2000 the number had been reduced to just 10.5 percent. For 60 percent of beneficiaries the benefits are over half of their income and for one third it is over 90 percent. Over 60 percent of beneficiaries are women who generally have less income than men (AARP, 2004). Also Social Security provides a foundation on which many private retirement plans are based.

Most laissez-faire conservatives have never supported Social Security as they believe that incentives are lost when individuals are not responsible for their own future security either by personal savings or purchasing retirement benefits in the private market. However, the program had been regarded as a success, until recently when conservatives have worked to hold down its expansion. With the growing political power of conservatives, it has been under attack more than at any time in its history. The goal of conservatives is to replace Social Security with a system of private personal savings accounts and private pensions and retirement plans provided by insurance companies and investment firms (McFadden, n.d.).

To move into this, the George W. Bush administration, with conservative support launched a major effort to allow persons to divert a portion of Social Security payroll tax to their own personal retirement accounts that would be managed by investment firms. The claim was that private investment would produce greater returns and hence, greater security. Conservatives attack Social Security on the basis that due to the baby boom the Trust Fund will not have enough funds to pay promised benefits when they retire. Analysts state the Trust Fund will grow to $3.7 trillion by the end of 2022, and will have enough funding to pay promised benefits to the year 2036. After that the benefits will have to be reduced to 77 percent of the promised benefit (Board of Trustees of the Federal Old-Age and Survivors Insurance and Federal Disability Trust Funds, 2011). There are numerous proposals to remedy this situation. The main proposals are to take the cap off the payroll tax of

$106,800 for 2011 and accelerate raising the retirement age to 68 years-old-to deal with the increase in life expectancy. The cap was taken off the payroll tax for Medicare without raising undue concerns and it would seem possible to do the same for retirement benefits. Keeping the early retirement at age 60 with reduced benefits should continue to allow individuals who want to retire early or work a less strenuous job. Also, widow benefits should continue to be paid at age 60 for those who are not working or receiving their own benefits. Confusion about Social Security was created when in 1969, under President Johnson, the Trust Fund was included in the government surplus, and falsely implying that the deficit was taking money out of the Trust Fund. What should have been pointed out is that the Trust Fund is there to pay Social Security benefits, is not a part of the surplus, and that without including it the actual deficit is higher. This "unified budget" approach, a measure of the federal budget in which every function and activity of government is added together to assess the federal budget, was used by all presidents from 1969 to 1986. It was not until 1990, that the Omnibus Budget Reconciliation Act (OBRA) stopped the use of the Trust Funds in the deficit calculations (DeWitt, 2005).

Those defending Social Security pointed out that many of its security features would be lost by shifting to IRAs, one being that the adequacy of personal savings accounts would depend on how long the beneficiary and his or her spouse lived (Kingson, 1996). Also the values of investments tend to be unstable and fluctuate from year-to-year depending on the stock market and the economy, and do not necessarily respond to changes in the cost of living. It is very sad when persons cannot retire as planned due to a drop in the value of their retirement account. Also fees have to be paid to investment firms for managing the account from which they make substantial profits. Under Social Security, one can receive full benefits after only10years of covered employment. This protects many women and others who for various reasons have not worked all their lives as most would not be able to save an equivalent amount in the time that they worked. Further, divorced spouses who are entitled to spouse and widows benefits under Social Security, would find it difficult to collect any benefits from the retirement accounts of their former spouses.

The social insurance system in general and Social Security in particular is one of the most effective method of achieving the goals of social justice in that they provide economic security for all covered persons by means of mutual aid and shared risks. The great strength of Social Security is that it pays a benefit to all regardless of other income and hence, does not divide the wealthy and the middle class from the low-paid laborer and the poor, where racial and ethnic factors can play a part. As such it is the very foundation of the social welfare system and the Social Security Act that has been regarded as the Magna Carta of the U.S. social welfare system. Hence the battle to save Social Security can be thought of as the critical battle for economic security and social justice. If lost, it will foster an erosion back to the centuries old system of the Poor Law that provided only the most basic safety net protection, often in a punitive environment that blamed the victim. It would be a mistake to underestimate the strength of the opposition to Social Security. The opposition has millions to spend on elections, in marketing its position, and can claim considerable media support. Those supporting the Social Security system must be especially aware that it avoids blaming the victim for unemployment and poverty, and hence being held responsible for their own security.

Most experts feel that a defined lifetime benefit provided by Social Security must be the rock on which basic retirement security is built and that individual retirement accounts should be an add on. With many employers replacing their defined benefit pensions with an individual retirement account, there might be consideration of giving employees the choice of an individual retirement account or a defined retirement insurance benefit to add to their Social Security benefit. This would be financed by payroll deductions to which employers might contribute. This add on might be administered by the Social Security Administration at little additional cost. As is the case with the current Social Security Trust Fund, this could be invested in government bonds that would retain their value regardless of economic factors and would provide real security. A big problem with employer provided retirement systems is that they are endangered by changes in ownership and loss of jobs. Under this proposal, coverage would continue when one moves jobs, as is the case with the current national Social Security system. An add on to Social Security could include coverage for private retirement accounts. There would be a choice for a private defined benefit pension that an insurance company might offer, and an add on to the Social Security benefit that could provide greater protection at a lower cost.

Means Tested Social Welfare Programs

The most traditional form of social welfare is where eligibility is "means tested," where the person or family does not have the means (mostly income) for basic essentials that they are judged to need. The advantage of means-tested systems is that they are the least costly and efficient in that aid is provided where it is most needed. The clear disadvantage is that it segregates out the poor so that those who do not see themselves, relatives, friends, or neighbors as at risk for becoming poor do not see it in their self-interest to support. This idea is reinforced by racial and ethnic disparities between wealthier groups and the poor. This often makes it politically expedient to blame the poor for their condition. Hence it justifies punitive and oppressive policies that serve to enhance the social dominance needs of everyone else not by lifting the poor up and instead by pushing the poor down. In fact, the constitutionality of these welfare programs has been based on the police power of governments to protect the safety and morals of the community that sees poor relief as a way to reduce theft, crime, riots and other forms of disorder that the poor might employ.

The means tested programs can provide flexibility in where it sets the income levels for eligibility, particularly as meeting certain needs that are more costly. The best examples are the rising cost of medical care, health insurance, housing, and childcare that are straining the budgets of many moderate and low-income persons and hence must be subsidized using a higher figure for income eligibility. Consequently, eligibility is set at various levels such as 150 or 200 percent of the poverty line. Providing subsidies for the working poor is a way of countering providing benefits just to those who have not worked to earn them. Similarly, fees for such services such as childcare and certain health services can be set on the basis of a sliding fee based on income.

There are other problems with eligibility for means tested services including how much wealth and assets a recipient should be allowed to keep. This is especially an issue in payment for large health care costs such as nursing home care. Another difficulty is the abrupt cut off when income exceeds the eligibility level, creating a disincentive to increase earnings. This bothers economists who think in terms of economic incentives and even refer to the reduction of benefits as a tax on earnings. Determining how much to disregard earnings and the increased cost if more earnings are disregarded create difficult public policy problems. Other problems are administrative, especially how to deal with special circumstances and changing economic conditions. For example, there are families in special circumstances due to high housing cost, debts due to student loans and the like, special family costs such as childcare costs or special needs of children with physical and mental handicaps. If all of these factors are considered in determining eligibility, the process can be quite complicated. There is also the problem that there is no incentive to report increased earnings that will lead to a reduction in benefits and may be only temporary. That helps to scapegoat recipients as frauds and cheats and to justify punitive measures such as time limits on benefits.

Public Assistance for Families and Individuals

Public assistance to families and individuals is a means tested program that stems from the English Poor Law of 1601, which required local parishes to establish programs for aiding all the needy poor that was brought on by the collapse of the feudal system of workers tied to the manor that provided food, housing, and basic economic security. The Poor Law was brought to the U.S. and administered by local governments. Basic aid given to persons living in their own homes was called "out-door" relief, and in aid given in almshouses and poor farms was called "in-door" relief. Aid was often given "in-kind" in the form of food, and clothing or through vouchers to purchase certain items and to pay the rent and utility bills.

Much of the struggle for social justice involves a journey from the Poor Law, with its meager safety net provisions and with minimum regard for human rights, to what has been called the welfare state, which seeks to provide economic security for all, not just the poor. In the U.S. this has taken place mostly in two periods of reform. The first occurred during the Great Depression with the passage of the Social Security Act of 1935 that in the name of social justice broke away from the Poor Law. The Act resulted in a revolutionary change with the use of social insurances. In the area of means tested public assistance programs, the Act broke away from the locally administered Poor Law by providing federal matching funds on a case basis to needy persons in the categories of aid to families with dependent children and the adult categories of aid to the blind, permanently and totally disabled, and those over age 65. The Act stipulated that this aid be "out-door"-given to persons in their own homes and in the form of cash. Most importantly, it established the concept of a state entitlement by providing that all eligible persons be served throughout the state. The Act set no standards for the amount of aid other than to require that states set up their own standard of need. Those persons that did not fit into the categories consisted mainly of able-bodied adults below the age of 65 not caring for minor children. They remained as part of the locally administered Poor Law, which was called general assistance.

The second period of reform was the 1960s, when the civil rights movement led to the "War on Poverty" that produced programs to make public assistance mainly a federal program that sought to treat poverty and aid to the poor as a national problem and get away from state and local constraints. One major achievement was that the adult categories of aid to the aged, blind and disabled were federalized into what was called Supplementary Security Income (SSI). SSI established a means tested supplement to Social Security benefits for those whose minimum benefit was not enough to meet basic needs or who had not qualified for benefits in the first place (Trattner, 1999). Administered by the Social Security Administration, and as with Social Security, the benefit level is federal. It is adjusted annually for the cost of living.

The 2011 SSI federal payment standard is $674 a month for single persons and $1,011 a month for couples (Social Security Administration, 2010). The problem has been that the federal level of benefits has been below what many states had been providing, so that states had to supplement them in order to maintain the level of benefits. Because the level of benefits paid through Social Security is in most cases above that required for eligibility for SSI, the number of beneficiaries has been small in most wealthy states, which give recipients little political power. Some states have reduced the level of SSI supplements by refusing to pass federal cost of living increases and using the increase to reduce the state supplement. This reveals a problem faced by means tested programs. SSI has been popular as it is a national program and relieves the states of some welfare costs. The level of the federal benefit should probably be increased to provide a decent standard of living. SSI has mainly been helpful to states in paying for community care for people with disabilities, particularly people with developmental disabilities and chronic mental illness who have not worked enough to qualify for Social Security benefits for the disabled. Many of these cases require special supportive living situations such as group homes that states must supplement and it would be helpful if the federal government would increase the SSI grant for these cases.

As has been noted the poverty program of the 1960s produced proposals to federalize means tested public assistance programs for families. There were proposals for a negative income tax that would aid the poor by an income tax refund that would establish a safety net minimum income for families. This led to the proposal of the Family Assistance Plan by the Nixon administration that would have established a national minimum income of $24,000 for a family of four. As it was proposed by a conservative administration, it looked for a time that this would easily pass. However, the benefit level was too much of an increase for the Southern states and was too little for the Northern industrial states. Also, it came at a time of increasing conservatism and backlash against the civil rights movement. Conservative forces opposed to the poverty program eventually defeated the Family Assistance Plan. A similar program was proposed by the Carter administration but in the face of growing conservatism got nowhere.

At the time, many advocates of social justice realized that the Family Assistance Plan probably marked the high water mark of efforts to provide economic security for families. Since then the growing conservative movement has been able to curtail the entitlement rights of the Aid to Families with Dependent Children program (AFDC). Originally AFDC was intended as a means of helping widows with children, but as life expectancy increased AFDC became more for the children of divorced and unmarried mothers, which greatly lessened its appeal. Also the caseload became disproportionately African American and Hispanic whose mothers were needed for the growing number of low-paying service jobs (Neubeck & Cazenave, 2001).

The increasing employment of women made it less acceptable to stay home and care for children. This led to efforts to force these mothers to work in what was called the welfare to work programs. That led to an emphasis on training programs to make recipients more employable that, as has been emphasized, was based on the concept of equality of opportunity. It only increased competition for jobs, resulted in blaming the victim, and a backlash against the welfare program by those whites who felt threatened. In the name of welfare reform, entitlement rights have been reduced and recipients deprived of a decent standard of living, as called for in the Universal Declaration of Human Rights, and that can only be viewed as an expression of the politics of human oppression.

Entitlement rights were removed in many ways. For example, the establishment of a family cap on benefits, which limited grant increases when more children were born, was designed to discourage mothers from having more children but amounted to punishing a child for being born and encouraged abortions. It also had racial overtones, being targeted to the increasing number of African American mothers on assistance who were unwed; it is appalling how the family cap has been accepted with little effort to repeal it.

Another development was to establish a flat grant on benefits in most states that varied only for family size. Previously the payment had been based on individual budgeting for families that considered actual rent and utility expenses. The result was that the flat grant was often too low for families to afford rent and became more so as rents increased faster than the cost of living. The result was that poverty and homelessness increased among recipients who were deprived of the right to affordable housing (National Coalition for the Homeless, 2007).

These developments culminated in the so-called welfare reform legislation of the Clinton administration that Republicans seized on in an effort to capture white votes. Congress in 1996 passed the Personal Responsibility and Work Opportunity Reconciliation Act that replaced the Aid to Families with Dependent Children program with the Temporary Assistance to Needy Families program (TANF). TANF virtually ended aid to needy families as a federal entitlement program. Federal matching of half or more of individual grants was replaced by federal block grants to the states not related to caseload, so states could cut their caseload without losing federal matching funds. The concept of a federal entitlement was abolished as states were no longer required to aid all eligible families. Worst of all, a five year limit was placed on the length of time families with employable parents could receive assistance, with states being permitted to establish even lower limits without making any provision for providing basic sustenance.

The TANF program also allowed states to establish sanctions against mothers who were deemed to not be making a good faith effort to find a job, and provided that recipients convicted of drug use be cut off entirely. TANF placed pressure on states to put more mothers to work on work for relief programs. These could be positive, depending on how much mothers were entitled to a grant increase for working.

These oppressive cuts were justified as a means to modify the behaviors that were viewed as the reason for recipients' poverty. The poor were seen as immoral deviants who did not try to become self-sufficient, had children out of wedlock, and abused drugs and alcohol. Informed persons would know that the poor are victims of the shortage of jobs, especially those that provide for a living wage, and that illegitimacy and addiction problems are not solved by punitive policies. Much of this also serves to enhance a stereotyped vision of African Americans as lazy and immoral (Alfred, 2007).

For many of those concerned with social justice, this legislation that deprives innocent children and their families of the right to a decent standard of living as called for in the Universal Declaration of Human Rights, represents the use of the politics of human oppression that enhances the esteem and dominance of groups, in this case mainly white workers and policymakers, by pushing down the unemployed minority poor. The main victims of these politics of human oppression are innocent African American and Hispanic children. This so called welfare reform legislation with its punitive and oppressive effects on child development and family life along with obvious racial and ethnic overtones should be seen as among the most infamous legislation ever passed by the national Congress and state legislatures. Sadly, the TANF legislation has enjoyed considerable popular support and there has been little attention to the fact that there is little evidence that those cut off got jobs that took them out of poverty or got jobs that would not have been filled otherwise and hence, failed to reduce unemployment (Cancian, 2001; Dorus & Robers, 2002; Sawicky, 2004).

Naturally the impact of lost human rights has been covered up. In the absence of official research, those who wanted to know were forced to contact these families second hand by locating them among the clients of homeless shelters and in training programs. In Connecticut, Manpower Demonstration Research Corporation (MDRC) conducted a study to evaluate the effectiveness of Jobs First, which provides cash assistance to families. Connecticut's Jobs First program assists families with an employable adult, and limits families to 21 months of cash assistance, with the possibility for an exemption or extension. Included were 4,803 single parents from two research districts: New Haven and Manchester. Of the participants 39.1 percent were African American, 22.4 percent Hispanic, and 37.6 percent white. Most were high school graduates, demonstrating that the level of education was not a major factor. The study revealed that those who found jobs because of Jobs First, initially worked part-time. A three year client survey found, most of parents were working on average 33 hours per week, with an average wage of $8.50. While some found jobs as a result of Jobs First, the program also produced an increase in the percentage of participants who reported housing instability and being homeless (Bloom et al., 2002).

A study by the Center on Budget and Policy Priorities (Parrott & Sherman, 2006) of what has happened in the 10 years since the passage of TANF suggested that its result has been to push most able-bodied unemployed off the welfare rolls using time limits, failure to make a full faith effort to find a job or by simply discouraging employable applicants from applying. TANF was established at a time of relative full employment when it was assumed that most unemployed pushed off the roles could find employment. The study notes that with the turn down in the economy since the 1990's, child poverty has increased signifycantly, as has the number of children living below half the poverty line. TANF now helps a much smaller share of families who are poor enough to qualify for the program than it used to. The number of single mothers who are jobless, do not receive TANF, do not live with others who work, and do not receive child support has grown significantly. Program participation has fallen among families poor enough to qualify for state benefits under the previous Aid to Families With Dependent Children program from 80 percent to just 48 percent under TANF in 2002 (The Urban Institute, 2006; Cauthen, 2006).

Without attention to these effects on human rights, the Personal Responsibilities and Work Opportunities Act that created TANF has been painted as a success. Hence, there have been limited efforts by social liberals and liberal advocacy groups to turn this around, mostly because the political climate does not support it. Clearly these oppressive cuts in welfare benefits need to be terminated, especially the family cap, time limits for those deemed employable, and for those engaging in what is regarded as immoral behavior. None of this should serve as a reason for human oppression, especially on innocent children. Further, welfare benefits should be sufficient to cover basic human needs. Flat grants especially need to be replaced with payment of actual rents and utility costs. There also needs to be provision for special needs such as special diets or special housing for the handicapped.

There needs to be consideration of more politically appealing approaches to aiding low-income families. One thought is to make more use of fiscal welfare that is popular with conservatives in that it uses income tax credits, deductions, and refunds. From the perspective of equality and uniformity, the best approach would be to adopt a federal negative income tax that would tax incomes above a certain income level and redistribute it by use of a refund to make up the income shortage of those with incomes below that level of income.

As efforts to pass the Family Assistance Plan in the Nixon years showed, the vast difference in standards among the states made it difficult to set the point of refund. With the power of conservative forces during the Obama administration a negative income tax now seems farfetched. However, there is a possibility to make more use of fiscal welfare by expanding the federal Earned Income Tax Credit (EITC) program and add state earned income tax credit supplements. EITC serves mainly to supplement low wages to help families provide for their children. It provides a refundable tax credit to those whose tax credit is less than they owe in income taxes. The program is also a way of relieving employers of responsibility for paying less than a living wage for families with children. As was suggested the level of benefit could be extended so that all families would have a level of income further above the poverty line. However, EITC helps only the working poor who have low-income or part time jobs. One easy way to help all low-income families is to make the child tax credit (CTC) of $1,000 fully refundable-as it is not now-for those who would qualify for more credit than they paid in taxes.

Often social problems can be solved by changing the definition of the problem. It might be helpful to define families with able-bodied employable mothers not as poor, but as unemployed. That makes it more difficult to blame the victim if one cannot find a job. This might entail having a federal-state program built around unemployment compensation that covers those with low incomes who have exhausted their unemployment benefit time limits, to which states could refer able-bodied employable TANF and general assistance recipients after unemployment benefits end. The welfare program would then focus more on employment and manpower development needs. For those who receive benefits for a period, there could be training programs or work offered on work relief or work for relief projects. Permitting the states to refer able-bodied TANF and general assistance cases would relieve an individual's dependency on public assistance programs, reduce case load and expenditures, and make recipients less of a target for punitive and oppressive blaming the victim policies. Federal matching funds could be provided on a case basis that would make it more of an entitlement as was true before TANF.

Another policy action to help families that has been more developed in other nations is to develop a national program for collecting child support for children deprived of parental support due to divorce, separation or not being married. Australia has established a national program that sets up a federal child support agency to which all families needing child support can apply and receive an order for child support. The amount of the order is based on the supporting parent's ability to pay. The strength of the program is that it does not require a court order as the result of a divorce or separation action and those required by the child support agency to pay support can appeal to the courts if they feel the order is not warranted. The order can then be sent to the employer to require them to withhold the support payments from the employee's pay. In Australia the order is sent to the national taxation agency for withholding that covers persons living in other states (Australian Government, 2008).

Here in the U.S., this could take the form of federal legislation encouraging states to establish similar child support agencies and make use of the federal Internal Revenue Service to order employers to withhold payments. The strength is the focus on the needs of all children rather than just focusing on reducing the costs of public assistance to the poor. If the U.S. were to establish a national child support collection program that applied to all, not just the poor, there might be a large constituency for adopting this.

Other actions could be considered for providing more income for children. One idea is to establish fatherless child insurance as a part of Old Age, Survivors, and Disability Insurance under Social Security. That would provide benefits in the event of divorce, separation, or death of a parent (Schorr, 1966). The problem is that insurance is best suited to cover events that persons do not willfully seek such as death, illness and unemployment. Divorce is more of a willful action, and therefore could be regarded as a means for increasing divorce, but this is something that could be piloted to see what actually happens. Other programs could be expanded that help provide economic security for families. One that has been suggested would be to include paid sick leave as an insurance benefit, perhaps connected with unemployment insurance. Another possibility is to expand payments of a family allowance for parents in fulltime education and training programs.

A bigger challenge might be to pass a constitutional amendment or legislative action to provide for the basic human rights of children and their families. In this regard there was an effort in Connecticut to amend the state constitution to establish that all children had the right to basic sustenance. This sought to build on a decision of the State Supreme Court that all children had the right to an equal education and hence there had to be racial integration of the schools. In seeking the children's rights amendment it was pointed out that the right to an equal education was greatly diminished if children did not first have the right to basic sustenance. The value of a constitutional amendment is that it gets the courts in addition to the legislature and governor involved in implementation. The amendment was too big a change for most, and some feared it would be interpreted as anti-abortion. Hence, it required a real organized effort that was not mustered and without which it did not pass the legislature to get on the ballot.

Another effort in this direction might be to pass a law giving children the right to sustenance and to authorize a special children's agency to study where children's rights were not being met and make recommendations for legislative action. Most state constitutions provide for the right to an education, but the economic right to basic sustenance has not been considered a constitutional right in a culture based on individual responsibility and on a survival of the fittest. Thus one of the challenges in the struggle for social justice would be to include in federal and state constitutions the human right to economic security that is included in the Universal Declaration of Human Rights.

In addition to providing financial assistance, the Universal Declaration of Human Rights calls for the provision of necessary social services. One vital social service is the provision of childcare for the children of working mothers. As childcare becomes more costly, this calls for the subsidy of childcare costs for which federal and state funds are available. Parents need to be charged a sliding fee based on income. Ideally, to meet the need, families should receive a subsidy with incomes below 400 percent of the federal poverty level. The shortage of funds for childcare subsidies continues to be a serious problem. In some states grandparents or other relatives can receive payments for providing kinship care that helps cover expenses of raising a child (National Conference of State Legislatures, 2008). Another needed social service is subsidized transportation services for parents to get to jobs where sufficient public transportation is not available. There also needs to be outreach social services to counsel families about family problems including financial management and to provide crisis intervention and information and referral services.

Chapter 5

Welfare Programs to Provide
For Special Needs

Nutrition Programs

A basic response to deal with poverty has always been to provide food to get away from the horrible image of persons suffering from malnutrition or starving to death. Pictures on television of children suffering from malnutrition in the South stimulated the passage of the federal food stamp program. Many churches like to respond to poverty by operating soup kitchen or food pantries. A lot of these efforts could best be called operating bird feeders, as they serve the social dominance needs of the givers by watching those being fed or receiving food to take home, rather than making any significant impact on the nutrition needs of families. It must be pointed out that most charitable actions are as much for the public image of the givers as caring persons as for the benefit of recipients and that charity rarely substitutes for justice.

Social justice objectives are more effectively served by the federal food stamp program, now know as Supplemental Nutrition Assistance Program (SNAP), which is a totally federally funded means tested entitlement program. This became a federal program with national eligibility requirements partly because it was connected to the national farm surplus program that got started as a means of disposing of surplus agricultural commodities. This evolved into a food stamp program that now provides food vouchers to persons with incomes below 130 percent of poverty and hence is targeted to the poor. The allotment is based on the federal thrifty food budget that is adjusted annually for the cost of living. The thrifty food budget is what is considered as essential for nutritional needs. Between October 2010 and September 2011 the maximum monthly SNAP allotment for a family of three was $526 and $200 for single persons (U.S. Department of Agriculture, 2010).

In 2009 the food stamp program was renamed the Supplementary Nutrition Assistance program (SNAP). The food stamp program has been a core element in the provision of basic human rights as it is non-categorical and provides for all individuals and families who have little or no income including those with low-income, part-time jobs, the aged, sick and unemployed. It has become virtually the only entitlement provision for many able-bodied unemployed persons who have been cut off public assistance programs. It is significant that the SNAP program introduced a categorical element that allows states to use their TANF funds to increase eligibility of SNAP to 185 percent of poverty. As TANF is a categorical public assistance program serving only single parent families with children this seems an apparent effort to respond to the oppressive effects that TANF cuts are having on the rights of children.

The SNAP program also abolishes a limitation on assets that recipients may have so as not to discourage savings. The program is administered by the federal Department of Agriculture rather than by the Department of Health and Human Services. To some extent, this hides it as a social welfare expenditure. It is assumed that poor persons need to spend a third of their income on food so SNAP allotments are reduced by one dollar for every three dollars of earned income. The program has been credited with making a major improvement in the nutrition of the poor. When the rate of infant mortality was used as an indicator of the standard of living of a nation, the U.S. was revealed as having a higher (higher) rate than many developed countries in Europe and Asia. This led to the establishment of the Women, Infants and Children (WIC) program that provides extra nutritional food to pregnant women, new mothers, infants and children certified as having special needs.

There are ways to improve the SNAP program. As the costs of rent, heat, and electricity have gone up, families are forced to pay a larger portion of their income for these items and are dipping into food budgets. Hence it would make sense to multiply the thrifty food budget by four instead of three to establish the federal poverty line that is used to determine the income level for eligibility and that reduce food stamp allotment by one dollar out of every four of income instead of every three. The SNAP program considers rising cost of living, and therefore increases the allotment for those who are spending more than half of their income on housing. Also, as the poverty line establishes the minimum income needed for survival, SNAP allotments should not be reduced until income reaches the poverty line. This would contribute more to relieving poverty.

Housing Programs

One of the main challenges in dealing with human rights has been the right to affordable housing. That has become more difficult due to the rise in the cost of housing, growing conservative power, and the struggle for civil rights. Decent affordable housing is an essential human need as it provides protection from the elements and other dangers, and is also vital for health, to reduce incidences of asthma and lead paint poisoning, for example. It is also important for family life. Human identity depends greatly on where one lives. It is a source of security and stability in family life that when destabilized particularly affects child development and school progress (Cattaneo, Galiani, Gertler, Martinez, & Titiunik, 2009). Homeownership is a great aid to security and stability and to a sense of belonging. Hence a growing problem for many low-income families depriving them of the basic human right to housing due to the inability to afford homeownership or rental payments in the face of increased costs and oppressive welfare cuts. It should

116

be clear that the right to housing is not met by temporary care in a homeless shelter.

There are numerous forces working against the right to affordable housing. One is that where one lives is one of the most basic status symbols. Harriet Beecher Stowe (1852) titled her seminal work "Uncle Tom's Cabin" as an indicator of his slave status. Social status needs also apply to the neighborhood where one lives. This has led to zoning requirements to keep moderate and low-income housing out of certain areas. Restrictive zoning serves to keep a wealthy tax base for the support of schools and other public services, and has been a real barrier to the development of low income housing.

Forces seeking urban renewal and development of central city areas, primarily to preserve and enhance real estate values, have given a lot of emphasis to the social economic mix (John D. and Catherine T. MacArthur Foundation, 2005; U.S. Department of Housing and Urban Development, n.d.). In this connection, they have sought to demolish low-income housing projects, mainly those serving African Americans, and replacing them with mixed income housing. There has been little sense of responsibility to provide affordable housing for those displaced (Tracy, 2008). Developers have even sought to subsidize high-income housing.

The need for housing in order to attract workers for industrial and commercial developments and for community service jobs is putting pressure to provide moderate affordable housing. In these conservative times, state and federal funds provided for moderate and low-income housing have been substantially reduced, but this growing need for community development may help to turn this around. Another factor has been the need to care for the elderly, sick and mentally and physically handicapped in the community, rather than in expensive institutions and nursing homes. Thus an increasing number of housing programs are directed to providing homes to serve these groups.

117

In looking at public policies to make housing more affordable, there is a need to deal both with demand and supply. On the demand side, there can be various means to lower the housing costs to the buyer such as rent subsidies, lower interest charges, and tax deductions. However, these can lead to increases in the sale or rental price that sellers and landlords can charge. This requires dealing with the supply of lower priced housing units. The rise of housing costs is weakening the effectiveness of various methods of helping buyers with financing and other costs. Often people have been given rent subsidy vouchers only to find that even with them there is little that they can afford where they want to live. Hence there also needs to be an increase in the supply of affordable housing.

One problem is that the supply of land is limited and the market economy rations it by price, so especially in urban areas the price of land has substantially increased. This has led to calls for efforts to lower prices of housing units through more intensive use of land by the construction of high-rise housing projects. Generally private developers cannot afford to do this and charge affordable rents. Hence, the U.S. needs to find ways to use public funding to increase the supply of affordable housing especially in urban areas.

On the demand side, there are programs to increase homeownership by lowering the cost for the buyer. Here the main effort has been to lower mortgage costs. One is using fiscal welfare that provides a federal income tax deduction for interest payments on home mortgages that also applies to most state income taxes. This deduction has been sought by banks and realtors to foster homeownership and has been by far the largest subsidy of housing costs. This provides more help for wealthy families who are in high tax brackets, paying high interest costs, and at times own more than one home. As there is little evidence that this deduction increases homeownership there have been proposals to limit the amount of the deduction or abolish it, and use the additional tax income for other forms of housing aid.

Other programs have sought to provide more low interest mortgage loans. The housing industry is largely financed by the mortgage industry, which is a major factor in the functioning of economy. The Federal Reserve Board has sought to deal with inflation and economic growth by controlling interest rates and otherwise regulating the mortgage industry. The mortgage industry is facilitated by the quasi-federal agencies of Freddie Mac and Fannie Mae, which buy up mortgages from banks and bundle them for sale like stocks and bonds. These agencies own over half of mortgages that provide banks with the funds needed to make more loans, and serves as a major stimulus to the housing industry. One consequence is that prior to the 2008 recession, there was a housing boom and banks made too many risky, "sub-prime" mortgage loans that Freddie Mac and Fannie Mae purchased. When borrowers failed to make payments, stock holders bore much of the loss. In September 2008 Congress decided to deal with this by nationalizing Freddie Mac and Fannie Mae and buying up their securities so as to provide the banks with more funding to make mortgage loans. There needs to be tighter controls to avoid making risky loans, especially the use of adjustable rate mortgages that many moderate and low-income borrowers cannot afford.

Another core government program to foster homeownership has been the Federal Housing Administration (FHA) program. The FHA insures mortgage loans and hence enables more low-income persons to qualify for loans. This program has been more restricted following the 2008 recession and needs to be expanded. Another federal program that lowered interest rates for certain special needs groups was the G.I. mortgages given to veterans of World War II and aid to handicapped persons. There are also public and private programs to help with down payments and closing costs.

The main problem on the demand side is the inability of low-income families to pay the increasing cost of rental housing that constitutes a challenge in providing affordable housing as a right. According to the National Low Income Housing Coalition (2010), in Connecticut one needed to earn $47,843 annually or about $25 an hour to afford a two bedroom apartment. About 56% of Connecticut's renters are unable to afford rent for a two bedroom at fair market rent. The result is that many are paying more than half of their income for rent, causing real financial hardships and putting families in a survival mode under constant stress. The problem has been worsened by the use of flat grants in welfare payments that vary only by family size and do not consider actual rent paid. For many the welfare grant does not even cover rent so that, other than food stamp vouchers, there is nothing left for other expenses, causing suffering and homelessness. Some of these renters are able to obtain rent subsidy vouchers that help, but this does not meet the goal of providing affordable housing as an entitlement to meet basic human needs. Thus, flat grants are another form of oppression of those on welfare and there is a need to return to paying actual rents and utility costs up to a maximum.

The main response to high rentals has been the rent subsidy programs, the main one being the federal Housing Choice Voucher Program commonly known as Section 8, which provides a subsidy to families who pay more than 30 percent of their gross family income for rent. A subsidy voucher is given for the difference between the 30 percent of gross income and the actual rent paid, which must be no more than the standard rent for a moderately priced rental unit in the area. To be eligible a family's gross income must be less than half the median family income in the area and for 70 percent it must be less than 30 percent of median income. Some states also have similar rental assistance programs that are much smaller.

The voucher program is usually administered by local housing authorities. One purpose of the program is to serve as a replacement of public housing. However, this does not increase the supply of low cost rental housing units. The main problem is that the number of rental assistance vouchers are limited and only provide for about a fourth of those eligible, resulting in long waiting lists.

Despite the growing need, there have been only slight increases in federal and state vouchers. Hence the big need to making housing an affordable right is to provide rental assistance vouchers to all eligible persons. To keep costs low, Section 8 should be completely federally funded as is the case with food stamps. Also, to lower costs, eligibility would probably have to be restricted, perhaps to families earning less than 20 percent of median family income who might be required to pay 40 percent of their income for rent. The Section 8 rental assistance program is now the largest item in the federal housing budget. Most advocates feel that in conservative times making rent subsidies an entitlement is not politically feasible and the best hope is to gradually increase the number of rental assistance vouchers issued. One possibility for making rent subsidies more of an entitlement would be to have it as an add on to other entitlement programs for all those that would be eligible. This would include those receiving Supplementary Security Insurance benefits (SSI), Earned Income Tax Credits (EITC), TANF, and possibly state administered assistance.

Providing more family income to low-income families through various social welfare programs would help with housing costs. SNAP provides extra assistance to families paying more than half of their income for housing. Rental assistance programs have mainly been developed as a means to replace low-income public housing projects that have generated opposition for concentrating together too many low-income families. The idea of the rent subsidy is to give low-income families rental assistance vouchers to find their own housing and integrate them into the community, so they are less concentrated and less singled out. However, often individuals and families cannot find rental units that the voucher can cover. It should be noted that there are also rent subsidies in connection with the supportive housing program for the physically and mentally handicapped so they can afford housing that fits their needs. There are also federal and state subsidies to cover the increasing costs for heat and utilities that are badly needed in the face of rising fuel prices.

The big challenge is the need to increase the supply of affordable homes and rental units. Unless this is done, one effect of increasing demand may be to raise prices. Most agree that housing programs must be concerned with the volume and quality of the housing stock. The extent of need must be addressed rather than making token responses. The supply side must deal with the cost of land, construction and rehabilitation. The global economy is leading to increased industrialization and urbanization. As a result housing costs are rising in urban areas throughout the world mainly due to the rising cost of land. A factor in dealing with land costs is zoning requirements, especially in the suburbs that exclude moderate and low-income housing. To build moderate and low-income housing some states allow developers to appeal to the courts for zoning overrides, which has been successful in many cases. Another effort being used in some states is to give communities subsidies for creating intensive use zoning that lowers land costs per unit for developers. Often in exchange for this developers are required to set aside a number of units to be made affordable (Progressive States Network, n.d.). That has raised a question of volume. The Connecticut statute known as the Affordable Housing Appeals Procedure requires that affordable-housing developers set aside 30 percent of the units for affordable housing for a minimum of 40 years after the creation of the development. Half of these units go to those earning 80 percent of the state or area median income and half to those with earning 60 percent of the state or area median income (Partnership for Strong Communities, 2010). This statute still does not meet much of the need for low-income units.

Another approach is the use of community land banks. In land bank programs a housing agency pays for a portion of the land costs, thus lowering the selling price. When the owner sells the property, the land cost subsidy is recovered and the agency holds on to the land, allowing for a subsidy to the next tenant, so the supply of subsidized housing is preserved. The land bank concept if applied to construction or rehabilitation of multi-unit condos or row housing could help increase the supply of affordable home-ownership units.

Another successful method is community redevelopment projects that seek to enhance the economic use of land. These programs have used a combination of federal, state and private funds to acquire underutilized and depreciated property for demolition or renovation that is then sold or leased to public and private developers for industrial, commercial or residential use. As often this involves demolishing or renovating existing houses, this creates an incentive to build or rehabilitate housing to accommodate new workers and to take care of those displaced. Unfortunately the federal urban renewal program has been discontinued, and most urban redevelopment efforts have wanted to increase high and middle income housing and get rid of most low-income housing.

There needs to be a requirement that when state and federal funds are used to demolish low-income public and private housing, these must be replaced by the provision of an equal number of units of low-income housing. In order to have more racial and socio-economic mix this could take the form of setting aside a sufficient number of units new or rehabilitated for rent subsidy to low-income persons. There could also be incentives to deal with inflating land costs by using public and private funds to acquire land that is conserved for later development. Another consideration is to deal with the "brownfields" problem. Brownfields are land that has been contaminated by industrial and commercial use and needs to be restored. It lowers the cost to developers if sellers are required to do this or if public funds are provided for this purpose.

The main challenge is to construct and substantially rehabilitate affordable housing to increase the supply. During the Great Depression there was substantial construction of public housing projects, mostly federally funded, that provided affordable rents to low-income families. Much of the impetus was to help revive the slumping housing industry. Most of the units were built in low-income areas and were intended to eliminate slum conditions that were harmful to health and family functioning. After World War II some public housing was built, and the low-income areas became more populated with African Americans who came to occupy most of the units. Hence, public housing became more unpopular as many felt that this concentration produced too many social problems and interfered with the development of urban areas as fewer whites wanted to live and shop there. Eventually many of the public housing projects in the central cities were demolished. Most new public housing was built for the elderly.

States have housing finance agencies mostly financed by allocations of federal tax exempt bonds that states use to provide below market interest rate loans to for-profit and nonprofit developers and to individual home buyers to provide affordable housing. There are always issues of how to allocate these loans, such as how much should go to financing moderate housing to facilitate economic development and how much should go to fund badly needed low-income rental housing. The state housing finance agencies also administer the federal tax credit program that gives tax credits to businesses who contribute to the funding of affordable housing.

The recent trend is to emphasize the construction of mixed income housing with a number of units being set aside for affordable housing. The concern is how many affordable houses or rental units will be provided in projects and how many will be available for low-income families? The federal HOPE VI program has been established to facilitate the replacement of low-income projects with mixed income housing, but it is modestly funded. A related development has been an emphasis on using public funds to subsidize the construction of moderate income housing by for profit and nonprofit developers who are provided with low interest loans, insured loans, and direct grants. This provides for some mix of private and public funds to lower the costs to taxpayers. Also the sponsorship by nonprofit housing agencies, many of which are church sponsored, aids in community support of subsidized moderate and low-income housing in the face of much resistance and is a way to involve citizens in social justice actions. Most of the private funding by nonprofits comes from foundations that view their function as leveraging public funding.

Since the return of federal budget deficits in 2003 there has been a substantial reduction of federal and state funding for moderate and low-income housing, including the provision of housing for the frail aged and physically and mentally handicapped (Rice & Sard, 2007; Partnership for Strong Communities, 2011). Nonprofits are eligible for federal grants to finance the development of supportive housing for those with special needs, mainly to physically and mentally handicapped, in the form of rental housing, independent living projects and the construction of small group homes with supportive social services. There are also federal loans for the construction of nursing homes and assisted living facilities.

Federal funding for new construction and substantial rehabilitation in conservative times has been considerably reduced and now is restricted to such programs as mortgage insurance for developers for construction of one to four units of housing that is hoped to encourage more construction of moderate income housing. There is also the home investment partnership program that provides small block grants to states and localities to use in partnership with nonprofit groups to build and rehabilitate affordable housing for rent, homeownership, or for rental subsidies. In addition the community development block grant program provides funding for localities. The program is mostly used for roads and utilities in connection with new construction and for buying up and rehabilitating deteriorated housing units. Most states have programs that issue bonds and lend funds to provide grants for multifamily housing and homeownership. Some states have special housing trust funds for affordable housing financed by the use of such things as a tax on real estate. The crisis in mortgage foreclosures has led to federal and state programs that refinance loans and acquire foreclosed properties, which may facilitate the supply of affordable housing.

The largest program to achieve mixed income housing is the use of rent subsidies to enable low-income families to move into subsidized moderate-income units. This involves the use of existing rent subsidy vouchers, and does not do much to increase the availability of rental assistance units. There is a need to expand rental housing vouchers and provide a certain number of units in new subsidized housing as rental assistance units that might be funded by local housing authorities. Supply has the most potential to increase if rental assistance is attached to a definite housing unit. The big question is how many units will be provided? The supply of affordable rental units for low-income families needs to be increased. The U.S. in 2007 had only 44 affordable rental units available for every 100 low-income renters (U.S. Department of Housing and Urban Development, 2010). The action by Congress in setting up a housing trust fund, as part of the Housing and Economic Recovery Act of 2008 for the provision of low-income units, especially rental units, is an important development toward meeting this need. The housing trust fund will be funded with some of the profits from the federal Fannie Mae and Freddie Mac programs. This is a helpful start, but other sources of funding need to be found. This provision of low-income housing units would replace in part the now discontinued federal program of providing below market rate mortgages to developers for the construction of moderate-income rental units in need of restoration. Increasing the supply of affordable housing will often require many sources of subsidy, including the provision of low cost land, low costs loans, grants, and real estate tax exemptions. There has been a trend to provide localities with federal block grants for housing in place of federal funding for specific projects. Federal block grants are a means of avoiding federal entitlements to meet the needs of middle and low-income persons. Housing policy basically has been a federal responsibility because of the high importance the housing and mortgage industries have in the functioning of the national economy. The mortgage industry is a key element in the banking industry that is overseen by the Federal Reserve Board. In September 2008, the federal government took over Fannie Mae and Freddie Mac to provide more funding for home mortgages. The foreclosure crisis in the home mortgage industry created a concern for its effect on housing industry and on the entire economy, leading to Congressional action to buy up defaulted mortgages held by banks and take other actions to remedy the situation. Most economic recessions greatly affect housing construction, creating the need for stimulus by increasing federal expenditures for affordable housing programs. All of this points to the need for the federal government to adopt policies that deal with the demand and supply of affordable housing through the use of monetary and fiscal policies of tax relief, borrowing and appropriations for such things as rental assistance and new construction.

One of the most difficult challenges in the struggle for social justice is to establish a right to affordable housing, which is hampered by racial and socio-economic factors. The need for social dominance by many persons often prevents the integration of low-income persons and certain racial and ethnic groups in the community, and this consequently hampers integration of schools. Many of the oppressive welfare cuts are aimed at depriving recipients of the right to affordable housing. Thus anything that can be done to establish affordable housing as a right needs to be promoted, including an amendment of federal and state constitutions or passing state legislation declaring that everyone has the right to a decent standard of living including food, clothing, medical care and housing. This might first be established for families with children.

Health Care

Another great challenge in the struggle for social justice is the provision of health services to all who need them in the most effective and efficient way. Societies have always faced this if only to provide for a healthy labor force, to prevent illnesses and accidents from causing permanent disabilities, and to control the spread of infectious and contagious diseases. Thus there is more acceptance of medical care as a right than the right to affordable housing. Traditionally health services were provided by private nonprofit hospitals and clinics (many under religious sponsorship). Such organizations used reduced fee and charitable contributions to serve those who had trouble paying costs. In cities with a high concentration of poverty there has been a mix of public and private facilities aiding low-income persons. For those health conditions that require special forms of care, state and county hospitals and institutions were provided care, especially for the mentally ill, individuals with mental disabilities, the tubercular, and the feeble aged.

The technological revolution of the twentieth century transformed health care. There was a revolution in diagnostic technology using such devices as blood tests, x-ray and imaging techniques, and fiber optics, and in treatment using revolutionary drugs, vaccines, surgical procedures, prostheses and electronic devices, such as pacemakers and hearing aids. The result of these technological advances was that health care became much more costly, but more effective, with a huge expansion of the health care industry that became a major element in the economy and a major source of employment. Health care also became highly specialized, with the need for specialized physicians, nurses, medical technicians, and specialized treatment facilities including specialized hospitals, nursing homes and home care programs. This resulted in a concentration of facilities in urban medical centers, creating a problem in providing for the variety of needed services in rural areas. The system became increasingly complicated and difficult to access, necessitating case management services to get the right patients to the right services (Irving, 2009; Rosenblatt & Hart, 2000; Smith, 2011).

The consequences have been that medical costs have soared for everyone and charitable funding by private sources is no longer adequate to take care of those who have difficulty with payment. To afford high health care costs, most individuals must purchase public or private health insurance or use the health insurance proved through their employer. Another option is the use of public funds to provide services directly or to purchase them from private nonprofit and commercial agencies. Rising costs of health care have resulted in rising health insurance costs so that more and more individuals and employers cannot afford the costs and hence, more and more families and individuals have lost health insurance coverage. This has resulted in increased pressure on state and federal governments to provide some form of universal health care that would be available to everyone as a right regardless of income. This puts pressure on funding by taxes and raises issues of what form this should take.

There are basically three ways to provide universal health care in various combinations. The first is to put emphasis on government funded health services or insurance programs in which the government is the single payer. The second method is to require employers to provide health insurance for current and retired employees. The third is to provide public subsidies to individuals and companies to make health insurance more affordable. Government funded single payer systems are used by most countries that have a universal health care system. In the U.S. there has been a long struggle to provide government health insurance for all, starting with its advocacy by the Truman administration in the 1940s. The struggle finally resulted in the passage of 1965 amendments to the Social Security Act that established the federal health insurance program called Medicare that provides government health insurance only to the aged and permanently disabled. A part of the amendments also established the federal and state medical assistance program called Medicaid that provides assistance to low-income persons and families to pay for medical costs including hospital, nursing home care, and outpatient care by physicians and other medical care programs. Medicaid is categorical and only covers children and their families, the aged and disabled.

Medicare is a federal administered and funded health insurance program. It covers all persons over age 65 and totally disabled persons who are covered by Social Security. Medicare Part A covers inpatient hospital care for 90 days per benefit period. For the first 60 days it covers the full costs of care and from 60 to 90 days there is a co-pay charge. It provides a limit of 100 days of care in a long term care facility for those getting treatment after one has been in hospital care for three days. It also limits inpatient care in a mental health facility to a lifetime 190 days. The rationale is that Medicare should not be used for long term care of the mentally ill who were being cared for in state and local mental hospitals.

Medicare Part A is funded by a payroll tax of 1.3 percent levied on both employers and employees. Interestingly, Congress removed the payroll tax cap for the Medicare portion of the payroll tax creating little fuss. Removal of the payroll tax cap should be extended to the rest of the payroll tax (including Social Security), so as to increase the funding of the Trust Fund to cover baby boomers, and prevent a drain on the Fund when they retire.

Medicare Part B covers most outpatient medical care including diagnostic and treatment services, home care services, and physical therapy and aids for the handicapped such as hearing aids if ordered by a primary care physician. It is financed half by premiums paid by beneficiaries and half by federal funds annually adjusted according to the costs In 2007 the premium was $93.50 a month for those with annual incomes below $80,000 and somewhat more for those with higher incomes. These premiums are deducted from Social Security checks.

When the amendment establishing Medicare was passed, it was assumed that Medicare would soon become universal. However, as the private insurance industry expanded in response to growing costs, private insurance instead became the major means for the provision of medical care and a powerful source of opposition to a government take over. An effort to establish some form of universal government health insurance was attempted by the Clinton administration, but was defeated by a combination the private health insurance industry, health care providers, and pharmaceutical companies, all of which feared more government control, and political conservatives who wanted medical care provided by the competitive private market economy.

There have been several additions to Medicare since its creation in 1965. One has been the Medicare Advantage program, which enables beneficiaries to join health maintenance organizations and preferred provider organizations that limit the choice of providers but reduces deductibles and co-pays. There is also the Medigap program offered by private insurers and employee benefit programs that help with deductibles, and co-pays and cover drug costs and other costs not covered by Medicare. An interesting feature of this is the establishment of a series of standard plans that vary as to coverage and co-pays and deductibles. Private insurers are required to offer one or more of the standard plans that was developed to eliminate confusion as to what various plans offered in terms of premiums charged.

Congress also established the Medicare Part D drug benefits program that is not included as a part of the Medicare insurance program. Instead it is provided by private insurers for plans approved for government subsidy. Each plan varies as to the drugs covered and as to co-pays and has its own premium charge that includes a subsidy. The amount of the subsidy varies according to the plan and according to drug costs in various states. There is a deductible of $265 annually after which there are various co-pays up to $2,499 annually after which there is no subsidy up to $3,051 annually. At that point there are major medical benefits with small co-pays. This so called donut hole was closed in the recent health reform legislation.

Medicare has been very popular with seniors as it covers most of their medical costs. A concern is what happens when the baby boomers retire and qualify for benefits that will drain what is accumulated in payroll tax receipts and will require more government funding for part B premiums. This probably will require more funding from general revenues. There is also an issue of whether to cover long-term care in nursing homes under Medicare, which is becoming an increasing burden for states under the federal-state Medicaid program. Also the prescription drug plan provided by private insurers is costly to administer and confusing to beneficiaries as to which plan to enroll. Drug coverage should be included in the Medicare insurance program.

There are a number of advantages to a government funded single payer health insurance system. For example Canada, which utilizes a single payer system, spends less per capita for medical care. Further advantages of single payer systems include;

1. All are covered, including those considered high risk.

2. Health insurance is not impacted by marketing costs, higher administrative costs, and returns to stockholders.

3. The single payer system is administered on the basis of what people need and are willing to pay through taxes, not on what produces the most profit for a company.

4. Single pay systems control costs by negotiating what fees to pay providers and mandating the use of managed care.

5. If taxes to fund the program are levied on individuals and corporations on the basis of ability to pay, this furthers the social justice objectives of achieving greater economic equality. In practical terms this would mean greater reliance of progressive income taxes on individuals and corporations that tax higher incomes at a higher rate and less on payroll and sales taxes.

The difficulty in having a universal governmental medical insurance system is that it would essentially put the private health insurance companies out of business. In fact, the main task in politically conservative times is to prevent the existing Medicare program from being privatized by turning it over to the insurance companies. Because of the difficulty in getting Congress to consider a single payer system, there have been efforts to get individual states to establish single payer programs. As a result, in addition to putting insurance companies out of business, the big problem would be that states in order to fund it would have to substantially increase taxes on individuals and corporations, affecting their ability to compete with other states in attracting businesses and industries. Thus other methods for providing universal health care by the federal and state governments need to be considered.

Several states have proposed requiring employers to provide health insurance or to adopt various means of making health insurance more affordable for employers and individuals by lowering premium costs or by providing subsidies. There are a number of problems in requiring employers either on the state or federal level to provide health insurance for employees. The main one, as was discussed under Occupational Welfare, is that this is especially hard on small businesses and those with high labor costs. Nationally, employer health insurance costs have risen 39 percent from $5,100 per employee in 2003 to $7,080 in 2008. This has caused many employers either drop employee health insurance or greatly increase employees' share of the costs (Towers Perrin, 2008). Most proposals for requiring businesses to provide employee coverage have included a provision that small businesses would be excluded and others, mostly nonprofits and municipal governments, would be allowed to join state sponsored health insurance plans. Some would give employers the option of buying into state sponsored health insurance pools. It is agreed that this would lower premiums for small businesses as insurers could offer lower premiums based on economies of scale, but it is less clear how much large businesses would save. States requiring employee insurance coverage have levied a small fine per employee, for failure to provide coverage, but that does not seem to be enough inducement to offer employee insurance. Also there is the possibility that more employers will avoid expanding coverage by hiring more part-time employees, treating more employees as self employed private contractors, or transferring work elsewhere, including overseas. To be meaningful, employee health insurance requirements would have to specify minimum benefits offered and not increase costs too much for employees through high deductibles and co-payments. There is also a concern about shifting a larger portion of the premium costs to employees, though this might be a way of making it more affordable for employers. Shifting more costs to employees might be more acceptable if employees received an income tax credit for their portion of insurance costs. Also employers for whom employee benefits are a high portion of payroll might be entitled to extra businesses tax reductions. It is significant that most nations that have established universal health care have used a single payer system rather than requiring health insurance coverage by employers, and there needs to be consideration of how workable requiring employee coverage is.

Another policy option increasingly being advocated for is the establishment of a government sponsored insurance pool that would offer a variety of plans that insurance companies could bid to provide. The thought is that insurers using economies of scale would be able to charge lower premiums and that market competition would further lower premiums. There would have to be regulation of the plans offered in the pool in order to provide needed coverage such as including drug costs, mental health benefits and perhaps some coverage of long term care. Regulation should also require preventive measures, such as use of screening tests for various types of cancer. It also should consider the inclusion of plans such as HMO's that save costs by a more integrated use of specialists by primary care physicians. The use of a government sponsored pool could be available to employers, the self employed and individuals. This is being tried in several states and is also being advocated on the federal level by proposals to offer the federal employees insurance plan to employers and individuals that want to join. The obvious concern is how much these pools will lower premium costs and make coverage more universally affordable. The use of a state sponsored pool in Connecticut did not manage to lower premium costs sufficiently to promote wide use. Hence, if premiums offered by insurance pools are to be affordable, there needs to be substantial subsidy for those who cannot afford to pay the premium even though it has been reduced. Insurance pools can be a part of what needs to be done to provide universal health care, but are not the complete answer. Along with this some states have offered a low-cost health insurance plan with some subsidy to lower costs. The question would be whether these plans should be offered to all takers or if subsidized, only to those who would be eligible. If available to all takers with a substantial subsidy it would be like a single payer plan in that it would eliminate competition by other private insurance payers. If eligibility is limited to low-income persons it would resemble other means tested programs such as Medicaid.

Some states, such as Massachusetts, are requiring that all persons have health insurance but unless there is a broad subsidy, this will be an undue burden on low and moderate-income persons who will be required to spend a large portion of their income for health insurance. This violates the principles of social justice. One reason for requiring everyone to have health insurance is to prevent persons from delaying purchasing health insurance until they are ill and need it, as insurers need to be protected from enrollees who have pre-existing conditions. Because of the cost to low and moderate-income persons it would seem that a better way is to provide substantial subsidies so as to make health insurance more affordable to all. There might be some penalty for pre-existing conditions such as a longer wait period.

If universal health care is to be provided in part by private insurance, there would need to be subsidies for those who could not afford to pay the premiums. One advocated method of subsidy of health insurance costs is to use fiscal welfare and give everyone an income tax credit that could pay as much as half of the premium costs. This was one of the main features of John McCain's 2008 presidential campaign, which proposed a universal tax credit for families and individuals. There would have to be extra means tested credits to low-income families for whom the credit would not be enough to make it affordable. The main advantage of the tax credit is that it would be a universal entitlement that lowers insurance costs for all and that uses the income tax system by providing tax relief, which appeals to conservatives. The universal feature is that the tax credit would apply to all and would not separate out the poor and hence, avoids stigma and should have broad support. Another feature is that it would subsidize all policies regardless of costs and would not interfere with market competition. It would allow more choice of health insurance plans and help persons who wanted more expensive insurance that provided more coverage.

The cost of the tax credit could be balanced off by income tax increases that would make up for the loss of tax income due to the credit less the savings that the tax credit would make in reducing other health care costs. A federal income tax increase may be more effective than having different state tax credit plans that would affect competition among states. Further if this were to replace employer insurance systems, employers could be expected to pay their share through the corporate income tax that would be fairer for small and labor intensive businesses. Thus the basic issue would be the size of the credit and how it would be balanced off by increasing individual income and corporation taxes.

Means tested programs have been used for a long time to provide help for health insurance and health care costs for low income families. Means tested programs have always faced the problem of providing benefits that are not earned, so conservatives have wanted to confine them to those out of the labor market, such as the aged, disabled, and children, and make only bare provisions for the rest through programs administered by local welfare departments. The increasingly recognized need for universal health insurance is putting pressure to expand means tested programs. The main means tested program has been the federal-state Medicaid program, established in connection with the federal Medicare program in 1965.

Medicaid pays for the full scope of health care services provided to eligible low-income persons and families who do not have enough income or assets to cover costs. It is categorical and only serves children and their single parents, the aged and disabled. The federal government matches from half to two thirds of costs depending on the per-capita income of the state. To receive federal matching payments, states must submit plans that set income eligibility levels related to those established for public assistance programs, such as TANF and SSI. States can be granted waivers to change eligibility requirements for special cases such as the handicapped. Medicaid covers most medical costs, inpatient and outpatient care, including most tests and treatments as well as most drugs.

Medicaid has become the main program for subsidizing nursing home care and medical care for the chronically ill and handicapped. The costs of these programs have been rising rapidly, and Medicaid has become one of the major expenses for state governments. States are putting pressure for federal programs to pick up more of the costs. One solution would be to include long term care insurance as a part of Medicare. The 2010 health care reform act made Medicaid less categorical and more universal by including able-bodied, non-aged single persons without minor children and adults in two parent families.

Another major means tested supplement is the State Children's Health Insurance Program (SCHIP) that was passed by Congress in 1997. SCHIP provided a federal block grant to states for uninsured children with family incomes above eligibility for Medicaid so as to provide expanded health insurance coverage for children. It covers only children, with the federal government matching from 65 to 83 percent of state expenditure. States are given a lot of leeway as to eligibility, but as the block grant puts a cap on federal aid, most states have established a maximum income at something above 200 percent of the federal poverty line. There are limits as to the amount of premium, deductibles and co-pays a state can charge. Administratively states could place it under their Medicaid program or contract with a private insurance company, with most states setting up some combination of the two. The fact that the program was restricted to children, provided as a federal block grant, and not an entitlement indicates how reluctant conservatives are to provide affordable medical care as a right and will take only small incremental steps toward universal health care. Some states, in order to deal with the growing number of families not covered by health insurance, have used their own funds to extend eligibility up to 300 percent of poverty including parents. Congress tried to expand SCHIP by raising the income eligibility level and including parents, but this was vetoed by President George W. Bush. It is clear that if medical care is to be universal, medical insurance subsidy programs must be greatly expanded.

Important in the provision of universal health care is the adequacy of public and private insurance coverage. Adequacy considerations need to deal with the length and types of the services covered, including: tests and treatments, drug, dental and mental health benefits and also co-pays and deductibles. Private insurance plans like to exclude high-risk persons, which diminishes the insurance aspect of shared risks. Hence it is important that the private plans do not exclude persons or charge higher rates due to factors such as age. To assure adequacy this would call for government approval of plans required for employers, those offered by insurance pools, and those that qualify for a subsidy. There could be a range of plans offered that would vary as to the extent and length of coverage and co-pays and deductions that would reflect differing needs and ability to pay. In order to avoid confusion with what various plans offer and so as to compare costs, it might be best to have a series of standardized plans that offer the same benefits, deductibles, and co-pays as is now done for "Medigap" insurance. Among the plans offered there might be some provision for joining health maintenance organizations (HMO'S) and preferred providers organizations (PPO's) that provide less choice of service providers but reduce costs. Means tested supplements generally offer one plan. In order to reduce costs, governments have sought to negotiate low prices with certain service providers, which restrict the number of providers, hospitals and physicians that have agreed to participate. The result is that recipients have limited choices of providers, and locations may become over crowded, less accessible and hence difficult to use.

Also, there needs to be consideration about controlling cost of the provision of services. It would seem that if there is to be a public subsidy of health insurance costs, this would require some form of price control so that the subsidy is not passed on in the form of increased premiums. The ability of government and private insurance plans to negotiate rates and prices paid to service providers is an important means of cost control that has been especially effective in dealing with for profit providers, such as drug companies and commercial nursing homes. Conversely, there is often the need to increase rates paid so that required standards for staffing and the provision of services can be met.

Managed care is another important means of cost control when third party payments by public and private insurance plans are involved. Managed care generally calls for a single point of entry where the health condition can be assessed and the most effective and efficient method of treatment selected. This is often done by primary care physicians and could result in more integrated use of specialties that would save costs and provide better care. In many communities, primary care facilities are being developed that provide physician services along with basic lab, x-ray and other diagnostic services and can be used on a walk-in basis. These can be a point of entry for hospital care and various medical specialties that would be used when needed. It would seem that similar mental health centers need to be utilized as a point of entry for those seeking third party payments for mental health problems that would channel services to where they are most needed.

Another form of price control is the development health maintenance organizations (HMO'S) that are a form of health insurance in that they charge a set fee for each patient enrolled that is usually combined with some co-payments and limits on the length of care provided. These agencies are also used as a single point of entry for managed care.

There also needs to be consideration of prevention programs, such as the public health model of prevention that includes primary prevention that reduces the incidence, the number of new cases, prevalence, and the number of existing cases of various illnesses. Secondary prevention deals with early detection and treatment and tertiary prevention with disability limitation and management. Much of primary prevention deals with living habits such as eating, drinking, smoking, exercise and safety that are beyond the province of health care services. Prevention programs need to be promoted by various devices such as education and safety regulations that public health agencies should promote and coordinate. With the development of an increasing number of high-tech products and services, there needs to be more attention to their safety. Secondary prevention that involves early detection and treatment is the province of the health care system. Here the development of new diagnostic technology creates a challenge to utilize and it is important to provide for periodic examinations and screening, especially for those considered high risk, such as children and the elderly. This includes surveillance during periods of risk, such as pregnancy.

By way of summary, perhaps the best possible means of providing universal coverage would be a combination of programs that would keep the single payer Medicare program for the aged, possibly lowering the age to 60 or even 55; then providing a federal tax credit subsidy for all medical insurance policies backed up by a federal-state means tested supplement to make it affordable for moderate and low-income families and individuals. Insurance pools could be included as part of the means of lowering the cost of private insurance, but would probably not lower costs enough to eliminate the need for supplements. Most authorities in talking about prevention programs emphasize the need for good pre-natal care and physical and mental child development services in the first three years of life (Shonkoff & Phillips, 2000). Modern technology has made it possible to detect child development problems in the first years of life and to provide corrective treatments that may reduce a lifetime of disability. Hence, in the name of prevention, medical care to this group should basically be free and funded by a government single payer program.

The health care reform legislation passed under President Obama, known as the Patient Protection and Affordable Care Act (ACA) is a very long and complicated piece of legislation that is to be implemented over10years. It has drawn strong opposition, primary from Republicans. In 2011, Congressional Republicans were calling for its complete repeal, which would face vetoes from President Obama. Part of the conflict with the creation of ACA was that liberals wanted a single payer system and pushed a so called public option as a part of the exchange, but conservatives blocked the public option. With many compromises, ACA passed with several distinct features that were to be implemented within the first10years of its passage. The first was to require all private insurance policies to eliminate requirements that restrict coverage, including coverage restrictions due to pre-existing conditions. To deal with this, the act required all individuals and families to have health insurance or pay a fine. This feature has been strongly criticized by conservatives who claim that it is unconstitutional and want to use it as a basis for repealing ACA. Other requirements state that there be no time limits or limitation on the total amount paid out to an individual, and that family plans continue to cover youths up to age 26. The problem with these requirements is that

141

they will increase costs and most of those now covered want some control of insurance costs.

One of the main features of the ACA is to require that most employers offer health insurance to their employees. Beginning in 2017 states will have the option of allowing small businesses with 25 or less employees, to purchase coverage through the small business health options exchange that will provide a tax credit up to 50 percent of premiums. Other large employers of 50 or more will be required to provide employee health insurance. Employees who lack coverage and those for whom the premiums, co-pays or deductions would be too costly could join a state operated health exchange with employers being required to pay $3,000 annually for all employees that leave the employer plan and join a plan offered by the exchange. This requirement is a feature of the Massachusetts plan and it is hard to predict how this will work nationwide. It will increase health insurance coverage for small businesses that now do not offer it, but there is the question of large employers in labor intensive businesses for whom, health insurance coverage would be quite costly and how many will elect to pay the $3,000 annual fine and have their employee join a health exchange. It is hard to know how much these exchanges will lower premium costs, but the tax credits should be an incentive to join. Many, especially laissez-fare conservatives are skeptical about how this will work and want the act repealed. Most countries that have universal health care have not gone the route of requiring employer coverage and have relied on single payer plans. Thus it may be that ultimately there will be universal tax credits for health insurance premiums as was suggested.

Perhaps the main feature of the ACA is to require states to establish health insurance exchanges that would provide group insurance for those who sought it that could include public employees, employees of non-profit agencies, and individuals without employer coverage or for whom the employer plan was too costly. Those covered by the exchanges would be entitled to assistance for premium costs on a sliding scale up to 400 percent of the federal poverty line. The exchanges raise the issue of how much enabling individuals to join group plans will lower costs. It could be as little as 10 percent.

Other efforts to help enable persons with health care costs is expanding Medicaid coverage to include parents of eligible children and individuals without dependent children that will make Medicaid less categorical as was recommended above. Eligibility for Medicaid is set at 130 percent of the poverty line. The ACA also provides funding for community care of the aged and chronically ill to keep them out of costly nursing homes. For the Children's Health Insurance Program (CHIP) the federal block grant will increase by 23 percent. There is the question of how much these subsidies will make health insurance affordable for all. The Republicans may withhold funding for increased federal assistance for health insurance costs and many may support just giving the states block grants to help fund their own health insurance exchanges and other programs with the federal government picking up the cost of the expanded Medicaid program.

Services to the Physically and Mentally Handicapped, Chronically III and Frail Elderly

Another challenge in achieving social justice is providing for those with more long term needs, especially the physically and mentally handicapped, the chronically ill and the frail elderly. Here the challenge is to maintain the maximum possible physical, mental and social functioning for individual self-fulfillment. In recent years there has been more attention to the rights of the handicapped, spurred by the interest in human rights. There have been movements to get the handicapped out of increasingly costly institutions and nursing facilities, where many were merely warehoused. This was furthered by the development of new diagnostic techniques, such as imaging, and improved treatments, such as tranquilizing drugs, that made community care of the mentally ill and mentally handicapped more manageable.

Community care was facilitated by the Supplementary Security Income program, which provided federal funds for income for the needy disabled. All of this led to the passage of the federal Americans with Disabilities Act of 1990 (ADA), which protected the handicapped from discrimination in employment and required that employers and public facilities eliminate architectural barriers, primarily to those in wheelchairs. The ADA was followed by the Individuals with Disabilities Education Act (IDEA), which states that handicapped children have the right to an education and requires schools to develop individual plans for the education of each special needs child. A positive factor in this program's development is that almost anyone can have handicaps: They tend to transcend socio-economic status and hence include both families of high status and community leaders who can become effective advocates for actions and influence policymakers.

The fact that handicaps can affect almost anyone provides a broad base of support that benefits advocacy organizations, such as the ARC (formally the Association for Retarded Children). However, there have been many problems, the main one being that programs for the handicapped are labor intensive, as many people with disabilities need individual services on a one-on-one basis. That has made services very costly. A good example has been the cost of transportation services for the handicapped to take them to medical appointments, special schools and community programs. Many communities provide special van services that can take wheelchairs, and often a special attendant is needed that can cost as much as $300 per person per trip. The community care of persons with mental handicaps, many of whom are seen as having uncontrolled behavior problems, can be upsetting to others and leads to opposition to residential care programs in many neighborhoods. Here there are concerns around how much and in what ways handicapped individuals can be integrated into normal community

144

life, e.g., how much a child with serious intellectual disabilities can benefit from being in a classroom with non-disabled children and what special services need to be provided.

There are distinctions between the needs of the physically handicapped and those with mental handicaps. Physical handicaps, including problems in walking, hearing, and seeing, are visible and can be dealt with by technological aids such as motorized wheelchairs, hearing aids, and magnifiers that help vision. Computers have been developed that can transfer spoken words to writing and vice versa. Mental handicaps, in contrast, are less visible and harder to treat. It can be stressful and difficult to deal with persons rationally who may have behavior problems that are hard to control. Mental handicaps such as autism and Alzheimer's are increasing. Treating these individuals can be stressful for caretakers, difficult to treat and require special educational and treatment programs.

Looking first at the education of the handicapped, IDEA requires states to develop a plan for the education of the handicapped and, in turn, states require local districts to develop their own plans that the states monitor and evaluate, as well as require improvements. Each school is further required to develop an individual placement plan for each handicapped student in which the parents are to be involved. There are efforts to integrate handicapped children into regular classes. That requires teachers to receive training as to how to serve handicapped children and classrooms to be provided with special aides. The underlying rationale is that school integration will aid the integration of the handicapped into community life.

There are many new technologies that help the physically handicapped with speech, hearing and sight disabilities. The challenge is in the education of those who have neurological problems, are intellectually disabled, are autistic, have cerebral palsy, and are mentally disturbed. Special teaching methods have been developed to deal with these challenges, including techniques that develop different parts of the brain to make up for parts that are not functioning due to either birth or developmental disorders. Behavior modification techniques have been developed to deal with behavior problems of the hyperactive and mentally disturbed. More teachers are being trained to deal with neurological problems, and school districts are being urged to serve this population. In order to provide these specialized programs, regional programs need to be established, though the transportation costs may be high. These special education programs are becoming costly for local school districts, and thus more state and federal aid is badly needed.

There are programs that help disabled persons transition to employment. Often handicapped persons need special job coaches to help them both adjust to the job and deal with problems that arise, e.g., determining whether they are suitable for the job or need a different one. Employers can get federal and state tax credits for employing persons with certain types of disabilities. In dealing with the employment needs of the disabled, the ADA prohibits all employers of 15 or more from discriminating in any way against qualified handicapped individuals. Employers are to make reasonable accommodations to the known disabilities of a qualified applicant that would not impose undue problems on the operation of the employer, so the applicant can enjoy equal employment opportunities. Applicants may be asked about their ability to perform certain tasks but are not required to submit to a physical examination unless it is required of all applicants. Persons with alcohol or drug abuse problems are not covered by the act. Agencies serving handicapped individuals provide employers with assistance in complying with ADA regulations. The act has been regarded as generally successful, with more work being needed to help certain employers.

There are federal and state vocational rehabilitation agencies that provide special training for the disabled that will lead to their employment, and provide them with special assistance in finding and adjusting to employment opportunities. These agencies in the past seemed mainly focused on the physically handicapped, spurred by the needs to deal with those wounded during wars. The problem of veterans who served in the Iraq war returning with traumatic stress disorders should help put more focus on mental health services as a part of rehabilitation. Many communities operate sheltered workshops for handicapped persons who are not suited for regular paid employment.

In order to provide for the long term care and management of the physically and mentally handicapped, the chronically ill, and the frail aged, there is a need for a wide variety of services, such as childcare, group home care, foster family care, special housing, assisted living, and various levels of nursing home care. There is also a need for a vast variety of human services, including medical and nursing care and supports from social workers and other human service workers for individuals and caregivers.

In housing there is a need to have single-family homes and apartments that are wheelchair accessible. There is also a need for congregate units for frail and more handicapped persons, which have dining, recreation, medical, and therapy services attached. A recent trend has been to provide housing with assisted-living services that include help with activities in daily living, such as dressing and bathing. There is also a need for retirement homes and apartments that can provide for various levels of care. Most of these have been developed as an alternative to costly nursing home care. Here there is a need for separate units geared to different levels of care. Especially for the mentally and intellectually disabled, there is a need for supportive housing that consists of group homes and apartments where there can be some supervision and supportive help such as counseling.

The provision of supportive housing raises delivery systems issues. The trend has been for construction to be provided by private for-profit and nonprofit developers, with subsidies from public funds for construction costs, and rental subsidies for those who cannot afford high rental costs. There also need to be payments from Medicaid and other medical insurances for the nursing and medical treatment aspects of the programs. Because of the unpopularity of public housing, there has not been much thrust for the construction of public housing units for the low-income handicapped. As was mentioned, the need to get persons out of large institutions and costly nursing homes creates pressure for the use of more public funds to subsidize these services.

All of this calls for a centralized public or private agency where needed services can be planned and coordinated. Most states have special agencies that serve the blind, intellectually disabled and mentally ill. For other handicapped groups and for the aged and chronically ill this needs to be provided by a state or local public social service agency, either directly or by contract with a private agency. Many of these groups need ongoing case management services that work with individuals and families to help plan these services, to monitor how various programs are working and to provide support in using them. Many individuals need ongoing social and emotional supportive counseling by social workers, psychologists and other trained professionals, both for the handicapped persons themselves and for their families and caretakers.

There are many delivery system concerns regarding the organization and funding of needed services. One need is the provision of income for the handicapped who live in the community. Disability insurance is provided under Social Security and on a means-tested basis through the federal Supplementary Social Insurance program, which is intended to provide for basic needs. There is a necessity to supplement these benefits in order to provide for special housing needs. Some employers provide disability insurance benefits, and there should be consideration as to how this insurance can be expanded.

There is also a question of where to draw the line between social service and health care funding. Currently Medicare and Medicaid cover nursing home care, group homes and special residential care, but not assisted living, which helps with problems of daily living such as dressing and bathing. Long term care plus medical care can be extremely expensive, costing up to hundreds of thousands dollars a year. Medicare only covers a maximum of 100 days of long term care in nursing homes, group homes or special residential facilities, so that many have to turn to the means-tested Medicaid program to cover the long term care costs that requires one to spend down most of their income and resources until the income for eligibility is reached. As this is especially hard on families with children, some states have sought Medicaid waivers to greatly increase the income eligibility level for these families. Most private insurance plans limit the coverage and length of benefits for medical care alone and do not cover long term care costs.

Most proposals for universal health care reform have advocated for greatly increasing the income eligibility level for premium subsidies. There needs to be special public funding without a means test for children with costly medical and long term care needs, such as those with autism. Badly needed is the expansion of long term nursing home care and community care programs under Medicare, so that persons do not have to use up all their assets before getting Medicaid assistance. Private health insurance is more suited for acute care than long term care, with its high costs for individual cases; and most plans, which historically have rigorously screened out persons with preexisting conditions, will no doubt try to skirt or compensate for contemporary laws that require coverage for people with preexisting conditions. Handicaps, chronic illness, and aging are problems that cut across class lines, so that advocacy organizations for these groups, such as the ARC, can draw on a broad base of community support for the provision of services. This is especially needed to win support for the heavy expenditures that school districts incur for special education needs.

Chapter 6
Infrastructure, Services and Education

Infrastructure and the Struggle for Social Justice

Infrastructure is generally regarded as services and systems, mostly public, that are needed to support and facilitate social and economic processes such as roads, public utilities, public safety, health, education, recreation, and financial services. It is here that social justice concerns call for people to be treated equally when their basic and essential needs are met. A good example is the need for affordable public transportation for those who either do not have cars or are less mobile. Affordable transportation calls for subsidies for both the service and for riders who require transportation to their jobs and to health and education services they cannot otherwise afford. There is a growing awareness of the need to build a sense of community by providing community services and activities for all to enjoy. They include parks, recreational and leisure services, community activity centers, and libraries.

Infrastructure is increasingly recognized as a key element in economic growth that depends on the adequacy of transportation, public utilities, educational and training services for workforce development, and credit and other financial services. Infrastructure services are also an important means for increasing productivity and environmental protection. The interstate highway system has enabled the cheap and fast delivery of goods. One big challenge is the use of inexpensive and clean energy in infrastructure services. Educational and training programs are vital in developing more efficient means of production and better goods and services. Another need that is increasingly obvious is to have a stable system of financial services. The provision of credit needs to be regulated so as to control speculative investment and other means of financing

150

to avoid a boom and bust economy that leads to recessions and unemployment.

The promotion of social justice calls for attention as to how infrastructure services are provided. One area of growing concern is deregulation or lack of regulation in rates for public utility services, transportation and financial services. One very basic concept is that the market system does not work where there is little choice as to price or to the goods and services provided. This is especially true in the case of public utilities such as gas, electricity, and cable and telephone services, where the consumer has little choice about who to use and there is a lack of competing companies, which results in little or no price competition. The best example is the need to regulate rates in water supply systems, where there is little choice as to use and it is virtually impossible to have competing reservoirs and pipelines. There have been recent efforts to deregulate electric power based on the notion that increased competition in the generation of electric power will result in more efficiency and lower prices. It appears very doubtful that this will work, as electric generating plants are very costly and are not going to be built if the results are to be overcapacity and pressures to reduce rates. Also, the increasing number of transmission lines will be costly and inefficient. Hence the result of deregulation will likely be higher rates for customers, not lower costs. It appears that the public utility system provides a very efficient low-cost electricity system and, because it is assured a profit regardless of volume, works to promote the conservation of electricity.

The most obvious example of what can result from deregulation is what has happened to airfares. For those who need to travel much over 200 miles, air transportation is now essential. Currently the variations in airfare have little to do with how far one travels but with how competitive the route is. Clearly air fares need to be regulated so that they more reflect the distance traveled, which is the main factor in costs. Phone and cable rates have been chaotic and so confusing that more regulation and simplification are needed. There also needs to be some control over rates for the use of the Internet so that they remain low and available for general use. The Internet has been a good means for low cost political organizing that needs to be preserved if we are to have fairer elections.

There are other areas where consumer protection is needed in the interest of social justice. One clear need is in the area of consumer credit, where too many low-income persons have been taken advantage of, as was brought out in the subprime mortgage loan crisis. Heavy consumer debt can overburden individuals so that they have less to spend for consumer items, which in turn hurts the economy. There appears to be a need to control credit card interest rates and to impose limits as to how much debt persons can have, such as requiring that at least half of credit card payments must be applied to reducing the principal.

The need for savings and the use of consumer debt would be reduced if persons were provided with more security—especially in the event of loss of income—by public and private programs that provide benefits for unemployment, sickness and disability. There is a need for honest accounting and financial reporting in order to protect investors, and for access to credit information files in order to correct misinformation. What is basically needed is more ongoing support for consumer protection agencies, and more legal protections that deal with misinformation and practices that take unfair advantage of consumers with regard to the safety, reliability, and effectiveness of goods and services, and to pricing, added charges, and refunds.

The Educational System

Like much of society, the educational system embodies forces that work for equality as well as for stratification and inequality. Those forces working for equality mainly seek equality of opportunity— that all children, regardless of their race, ethnicity, or socio-economic status, have an opportunity to develop their full abilities and to strive for high status positions. Equality of opportunity has been spurred by the election of the first African American president, Barack Obama—which many Americans thought they would never live to see—who was able to use the educational opportunities provided to him to develop his knowledge and leadership skills.

Education by itself will not change the demand for various strata of labor; and it does not follow that increasing the general level of education by itself will lead to more equality in the distribution of income, eliminate low status, low paying jobs, or eliminate unemployment. Stratification and inequality of income are sometimes intensified by the accepted need in society to educate and train persons for positions that require specific certification or a specific education level. The facts seem to indicate that, despite the marked increase in overall educational attainment in recent years, the national distribution of income became more unequal, as earlier noted. There seems to be evidence that, due to the demands of the labor market, many of those completing college were either relegated to jobs they would have gotten without a college degree or were unemployed—a concept referred to as "malemployment" (Harrington & Sum, 2010). The lack of sufficient education, as has been noted, is often used as a means for "blaming the victim" for unemployment and low wage jobs. It is also important to remember that the level of education of workers will not prevent high-wage jobs from being outsourced to other countries, where workers with the necessary skills can be found to do the work at much lower wages. However, a higher general level of education helps create a more flexible and adaptable labor force. This is exemplified by workers with the ability to use computers, which has led to more productivity and efficiency; when passed on in wages, it may produce more equality in the distribution of income.

In dealing with equality of opportunity, there is nothing more equal than all children in a community being served by public schools. One can remember attending classes when some of the children of the super-rich sat next to "home boys," who were living in an institution separated from their parents mainly because of poverty. But one needs also to remember that equality in educational opportunity rests on much more than the schools. There is significant evidence that race-neutral plans in school districts lead to an increase in school segregation, which results in a decline in academic performance among those students attending racially and socio-economic isolated schools (Spencer, Reno, Powell, & Grant-Thomas, 2009). This shows us how much socio-economic status and racism affect one's education. Unless these factors are dealt with, the benefits of an education will not be equal. For those concerned with social justice, it is especially important to note how much poverty, racism and ethnicity affect the equity of education. The poor, struggling to pay their rent, are faced with homelessness, frequent moves and lack of family stability, which interfere with schooling. Those faced with oppressive welfare cuts get the message that "you don't count and we don't care." They are left with a feeling of powerlessness and hopelessness and the belief that nothing they do will make a difference. Those faced with racism are left with the feeling that the system is rigged against them—a feeling reinforced by increasing competition from advantaged students, based on standards the poor cannot possibly meet.

Teachers working with these children have the constant task of building up their self-esteem and convincing them that they can make it. Hence, it must be remembered that the right to an equal education is greatly diminished if a child and his family does not first have the right to "a standard of living adequate for health and well-being of himself and of his family, including food, clothing housing and medical care and necessary social services," as stated in Article 25 of the Universal Declaration of Human Rights (United Nations, 1948).

For those concerned with social justice, providing equal opportunities so that each individual can benefit from his or her education has presented a challenge. This has led to an emphasis on compensatory education for the disadvantaged children, such as the federal Head Start program, to provide a special pre-school education, so these children can succeed in school. That program was weakened, however, by the advantaged also wanting pre-school education for their children. There have been special tutorial and summer programs for the disadvantaged, but there are also special programs such as advanced placement programs intended for the children of the advantaged, which keep them ahead.

A significant event in the struggle for equality in education was the Supreme Court decision in *Brown v. Board of Education of Topeka*. The court ruled that racially separate education is not equal, and that there needs to be more integration of schools, especially by race. Since that 1954 decision, there has been a special interest among those concerned with civil rights to integrate schools in order to provide for equality of opportunity. It is also recognized that racial, ethnic, and other forms of social prejudice are most effectively dealt with when children associate with different children in the task of mutual growth through education, and that these children will grow up to see discrimination by race, ethnicity or other attributes as unjust (Spencer et al., 2009).

The Brown case established integration of schools as public policy. The case clearly eliminated *de jure* (in law) segregation, where students are assigned to specific schools by race, but did not eliminate *de facto* (in fact) segregation, of schools being predominately segregated by race based on where the children lived. Hence, with the growing concentration of African Americans in central city ghettos, schools became less integrated than before, and integration has become more difficult to achieve. With districts comprised of more than two-thirds of students from minority racial and ethnic groups, it became impossible to redistrict or bus children within the district to achieve real racial and socio-economic integration. It was especially difficult to bus children out of their neighborhood schools, as parents paying high property taxes developed great resistance to having their children bussed into ghetto areas, and they even showed some resistance to having children bussed into suburban districts, which sometimes did not accept them (Rotherham, 2010).

In some states there has been action by civil rights groups and others interested in social justice for state departments of education and local school districts to develop measures to integrate schools, even across district lines. For example, in the state of Connecticut an effort for school integration led to a decision by its Supreme Court that segregated schools deprived children of the right to equal education as provided in the state constitution; and it ordered the state department of education to develop a plan to address this issue. But in the face of resistance to forced busing, the state has had to resort to voluntary efforts, such as establishing special magnet schools in central city areas to which whites would voluntarily send their children. Efforts to do this in Connecticut have not yet succeeded in getting a significant number of white children from the suburbs to participate. The main focus has been on African Americans who do not want their children segregated from the mainstream of society.

To further complicate matters, the U.S. Supreme Court has increasingly become more conservative. A 2007 case from Seattle, for example, ruled that children could not be assigned to schools solely on the basis of race, which signaled the end of forced busing to some. The best hope for more integrated schools may lie in the voluntary busing of children from the central cities to white suburbs that get inducements for taking them. It would seem important to not give up on establishing a variety of integrated magnet schools in the central cities, to which suburban whites would voluntarily send their children; but the best hope may involve establishing special magnet schools in the suburbs to which a portion of children from the central cities who volunteer would be enrolled. One concern would be what portion of central city children could be served by such busing to the suburbs, and it would probably be less than 20 percent.

Another hope for integration lies in growing integration in the suburbs, but minorities tend to concentrate in parts of the suburbs that are zoned for lower-income families, which raises busing issues. Part of the solution for suburban districts may lie in redistricting to get more integration, in establishing special magnet schools that would be integrated, and by giving parents choices about sending their children to more integrated schools. Such integration will be easiest to achieve in more affluent suburbs, where whites are less threatened by job competition from African Americans, and where the number of nonwhite children from more middle class families is relatively small.

Another approach to improving equality of opportunity for African Americans and other disadvantaged minorities is to use affirmative action to get participation in relative proportion to their numbers in certain school courses. On the secondary school level, this would involve affirmative action to enroll students with potential in technical schools and in college preparation courses. On the tertiary level, there is a real need to affirmatively recruit and admit qualified African American and other minorities to undergraduate courses that offer associate and bachelor level degrees, with a special emphasis in courses where minorities are underrepresented, such as in the physical sciences and engineering. There also needs to be special affirmative action to get African Americans and other disadvantaged minorities represented in graduate programs for the professions.

An equal educational experience also requires that there be special state and federal aid to school districts with many low-income families and a small tax base. Some have wanted to deal with the problem of poorly performing schools by allowing parents to enroll their children elsewhere, and even giving them vouchers to send their children to private schools. This raises the question of whether giving parents the choice of sending their children to other schools, both within the district and to the suburbs, would be sought by the more advantaged families, leaving the more disad-

157

vantaged behind. This would worsen the problem and call for some socio-economic mix in selecting children to participate. Allowing parents to enroll their children in better schools also blames the schools with many disadvantaged children, which really need to provide more remedial education or be a part of a program to use busing for more socio-economic mix.

There are examples of schools where strong leadership, teacher selection and special efforts have been successful in dealing with the problem of poor performance. They need to be replicated on a large scale. Some of these schools are charter schools that operate with public funds, but are given substantial independence in how they operate with a separate board. This development raises issues as it replaces the motto "good schools for all children," used by many social justice advocates, with "some good schools for some children." Use of charter schools seems most justified when they are either targeted to serve children of low socio-economic status or as a means of furthering racial integration. There are indications that some charter schools are used to pull the more advantaged out of failing schools; or for political purposes, such as a means of getting rid of teachers unions; or to affect selective admissions that favor elites and activists and exclude special needs children. Charter schools are heralded for avoiding bureaucratic red tape, but there is a danger that hiring teachers will become more political, favoring those with ties to certain board members, and that there will be favoritism in awarding contracts. There clearly needs to be public accountability as to how funds are spent and positions are filled (Vergari, 2007).

In the discussion of equality of opportunity, it seems helpful to reflect on the different responses of the laissez-faire conservatives and social liberals about the use of national and state standard achievement tests. Laissez-faire conservatives are strongly committed to competition as a means of providing better goods and services, and they feel that the education system can best be improved by competition in school achievement. Hence, they strongly support raising academic standards and challenging competitors to meet them. The result is that those behind can never catch up, in what has become a faster race. African Americans (boys especially), for example, find out that when they have succeeded in graduating from high school, the only ones they have beaten out for good jobs are their own African American brothers and some white "loser" types. The result is that equality of opportunity objectives are not met, and the victims of unemployment and poorly paying jobs are blamed for their lack of educational achievement. This can best be understood as the implicit, if not explicit, expression of the survival of the fittest ethos, which emphasizes achievement. The laissez-faire conservatives also blame schools, teachers, and unions for poor performance and underachieving schools, and many want to eliminate teachers unions (Johnson & Salle, 2004).

By contrast, social liberals feel there is too much emphasis on test score competition and that schools should improve in many ways. They especially seek to close the achievement gap between the disadvantaged racial, ethnic and low-income minorities and the rest of the student population. Social liberals want teachers with special talents to work with disadvantaged youth, with many special supports; and they want more recognition that education involves giving these children confidence they can achieve anything. Many social liberals feel there is too much emphasis on high stakes testing, and that schools should function more as places for human development, where children learn teamwork and how to interact to foster personal growth; are helped to find what is self-fulfilling and identify their talents and interests; and can develop means of expression—verbally, in writing, artistically, and through physical activities (Ravitch, 2010; Urrieta, 2004).

Access to Higher Education

Equality of opportunity includes more equality in access to higher education, where tuition and other costs have been rising faster than the overall cost of living. The main policy response has been the provision of student loans, with the result that students have become heavily in debt, and this has put real strains on low-income students. To address this problem the Health Care and Education Reconciliation Act offers protections for students who have difficulty repaying their loans. As currently written, students who enter college in 2014 or later are offered choices as to how they repay their loans: an income-based repayment plan where borrowers pay no more than 10 percent of their income above a basic living allowance; and debt forgiveness after 20 years, or 10 years for those in public service. In addition, the federal government more than doubled funding for Pell scholarships between the years 2008 and 2011, and tripled the American Opportunity Tax Credit for college students (The White House, 2010a).

In many countries, higher education is provided by public colleges and universities with very low tuition, and some countries have provided a cost of living allowance to students attending full time. In the U.S., tuition and cost of living allowances have been provided mainly for war veterans. There need to be more efforts to lower tuition costs in both public and private higher education, more Pell grants that provide scholarships to low-income students and more cost of living allowances.

In dealing with the relationship of social justice objectives to the educational system, it is important to remember that equality of opportunity deals with becoming more competitive in seeking higher status positions, and does not substitute for equality of outcome; and that equality of opportunity is used by the laissez-faire conservatives to justify the survival of the fittest ethos by making the competition more equal. In dealing with equality of opportunity, it is well to note that upward mobility depends on the number of opportunities to move up. In agricultural societies there are large numbers of farm laborers on the bottom, a few farm owners, business people and professionals at the top, and very few "middle income" positions. The result is that there is virtually no chance for farm laborers to move up by getting more education. Thus equality of opportunity requires the creation of more middle income positions in the occupational strata and potential for upward mobility, which an education can help to foster.

Most of those advocating for increased educational attainment as a major solution to inequality are basically using the equality of opportunity objective. As previously mentioned, there is little evidence that greater educational attainment by itself leads to more socio-economic equality, to a reduction in unemployment or to greater equality in wages. Educational attainment must be coupled with a healthy economy and job opportunities (Harrington & Sum, 2010). Though increased educational attainment is not the bonanza that laissez-faire conservatives would have one believe it is, the fact is that advanced and developing societies depend on a well prepared, adaptable labor force. Economic growth that is the basis for full employment and a rising standard of living depends on developing technologies for newer and better goods and services that are delivered more efficiently.

Accomplishing this growth calls for a focus on providing more education in the basic sciences, including the physical sciences of physics, chemistry, biology and botany, and the social sciences of economics, psychology, sociology and government, as a basis for professional and technical education. Industrial growth depends on educating scientists, engineers and technicians to develop newer and better products, and also educating workers to manufacture the products. This creates high-wage jobs that, for economic growth, need to be kept domestic and not outsourced to the extent currently being done.

Another crucial area lies in providing more education in medical sciences, including pharmacology, where technological developments are increasing the demand for workers. It must not be forgotten how much education in agriculture has led to new crops and technologies, in what is termed the agricultural revolution, whereby increased production with a much smaller labor force has done so much to relieve world hunger.

If social justice objectives are to be achieved, there also needs to be more education for citizenship, as a democracy depends on a well informed polity. There needs to be greater understanding of economic and social components in public policy decisions, so people better understand what policies are in both their own best interests and society's as a whole. There should be an emphasis on more education in human rights, in macro-economic concepts that deal with employment and wages, in the politics of the struggle for social justice, and in greater understanding of the psychosocial dynamics of social relationships. However, it needs to be remembered that the level of education can be a two-edged sword—on the one hand fostering full social participation while on the other hand excluding those with less education from participation in areas where they could make a meaningful contribution.

Chapter 7
Civil Rights and Civil Liberties

Fundamental to the provision for social justice is the elimination of discrimination of people for attributes of birth and other factors, such as disability, that are beyond their control. Articles 1 and 2 of the Universal Declaration of Human Rights (United Nations, 1948) respectively state:

> "All human beings are born free and equal in dignity and rights. They are endowed with reason and conscience and should act towards one another in a spirit of brotherhood."

> "Everyone is entitled to the rights and freedoms set forth in this Declaration, without distinction of any kind, such as race, color, sex, language, religion, political or other opinion, national or social origin, property, birth, or other status."

In defining the basis of social justice as equal rights, a distinction must be made between "protective rights"—defined as those rights protected from interference from governments and others—and "positive rights"—defined as entitlement rights, including economic rights to enough income for an adequate standard of living for one's self and family; to the right to economic security; to an education; to medical care and common infrastructure services; and to a stable financial system.

The concerns for civil rights and civil liberties tend to deal more with protective rights, personal rights of freedom from unjustified discrimination, and to privacy. The protection of personal rights and freedom is best suited to the ethos of laissez-faire conservatism, which focuses on the freedom to bargain in the market place, the exercise of consumer sovereignty, equality of opportunity, and freedom from interference by governments. This leads conservatives to be more concerned with protective rights, such as protection from child abuse, than with economic rights, such as the rights of children to the provision of basic food, housing, and medical care. Hence, the media have reported constantly on cases of child abuse and essentially ignored the effect on children of oppressive welfare cuts that deprive them of the right to basic sustenance. Another example was the use by conservatives, a century ago, of the right of freedom of contract to oppose any restriction on hiring child labor.

Civil Liberties

Civil liberties place emphasis on freedoms, including freedom of information, of speech, of the press, and of assembly. One of life's main struggles is the corporate and individual struggle for truth, which requires obtaining adequate and objective information. The essence of democracy is that the populace has freedom of opinion and expression. Article 19 of the Universal Declaration of Human Rights states the right "to seek, receive and impart information and ideas through any media and regardless of frontiers" (United Nations, 1948). In this information age, where so much information can be obtained through so many media sources, one of the main sources of power is the ability to control what information and ideas receive attention. Thus, those who own and manage the media have ever-increasing power. As many have noted, the increasing consolidation of media ownership has brought about increasing power, to the point where probably a few thousand persons in the nation have major control over what information and opinions are expressed in the media. One remembers how much William Randolph Hearst pushed the Spanish-American War and how much Henry Luce of *Life* and *Time* promoted the China lobby that opposed communist China (PBS, 1999; Brinkley, 2010). One countervailing force is the use of the Internet, which for most people does not require immense capital resources.

Those controlling the media are the owners of capital who have often embraced the laissez-faire conservative positions. They have especially opposed the trade union movement and, with that, the right to fair labor standards, a living wage, a job, economic security, and most entitlements. Hence, if the struggle for social justice is to succeed, information about its ethos, challenges, opinions and solutions must be imparted to the populace. One challenge is to keep the use of the Internet as low-cost as it now is for most people; another is to prohibit the number of newspapers, radio and television stations under joint ownership, as is done in many European countries; a third is more support for aid to public service radio and television stations, where there can be more debate that deals with different sides of public issues.

Related to this are concerns about freedom of religion. Article 18 of the Universal Declaration of Human Rights reads:

> "Everyone has the right to freedom of thought, conscience, and religion; this right includes freedom to change his religion or belief, and freedom either alone or in community with others and in public or private, to manifest his religion or belief in teaching, practice, worship, and observance" (United Nations, 1948).

As has been pointed out, the struggle for social justice rests on social ethics based on ethical and religious beliefs and, hence, freedom of religion is an essential element. This raises issues of separation of church and state. One concern is the provision of government aid for social services or education directly to churches through the White House Office of Faith-Based and Neighborhood Partnerships. Under this program, churches that provide community service may be eligible for government funding, on the basis that the funds do not support religious activities; that the religious activities conducted as a part of the organization be done apart from the community services, at a different time or separate location; and that the organization not discriminate who can use the services based on religion (The White House, 2010b). Even with the efforts of the government to protect the separation of church and state, there still exists a danger that churches receiving government funds for social services will proclaim their beliefs in preference to others. Another concern is that separation of church and state means that churches must be politically neutral. Generally this has been interpreted to mean that churches must not endorse or campaign in favor of a political candidate, but are not constrained in urging their members to be involved in public issues, especially those dealing with social justice and social ethics. In fact churches have always been involved in matters of public concern, the best example being their involvement in the abolitionist's movement against slavery. The recent effort to prohibit a church from publicly criticizing the president for the conduct of a war rests on thin ice, as it is clear that this would not apply if the president were praised for his actions.

During the Cold War, there were many efforts to stop churches from advocating for what were regarded as communist beliefs that affected social justice concerns. In response to all of these efforts, it is important that freedom to hold and express religious beliefs be upheld.

Another important area affecting social justice is privacy and equality before the law. The right to privacy is essential in preventing unjust interference in one's private affairs. Equality before the law deals with equal protection of the law and with due process rights. Equal protection is generally interpreted to mean equal protection of life, personal safety, health and well being, personal freedom, and property. This raises questions of what should be considered equal. Most agree that this should apply to indigenous factors such as race, ethnicity, and sex. More complicated are factors such as age, physical and mental handicaps, sexual orientation and, also, socio-economic status, where many—especially those with a more conservative orientation— would argue that equality does not apply and classifications may be made, e.g., by age. Here, because of evidence that the mind is not fully developed until the mid-twenties and that more behavioral problems occur among those in their late teens, there are efforts to raise the age that one can drive and drink alcohol. Other examples are whether drug addiction should be regarded as a mental handicap and, hence, not be a basis for incarceration, or whether same-sex sexual orientation should be regarded as indigenous or stigmatized as unacceptable behavior.

For those concerned with social justice, there are, or should be, considerations about equal protection in terms of socio-economic status. A good example, and one that should be debated more, is whether people should lose the right to basic sustenance through social welfare programs because they were found guilty of drug possession. It would seem that equal protection would require that they only be punished the same as everyone else and hence not lose their welfare grant. There are also concerns as to whether some groups are entitled to special protection, such as the protection being used for gays and lesbians who are victims of hate crimes, and protection for women who are victims of domestic violence by males. There seems to be real danger to the concept of equality if protection becomes related to the status of the victim and social dominance factors come into play. For example, there is often a lot of petty theft by homeless alcoholics, who are nearly defenseless and cared about by few, but social justice concerns call for them to receive equal protection. A related consideration is the application of equal protection when related to law enforcement, especially to racial and ethnic profiling in searches and interrogations, and to more intensive law enforcement in low socio-economic status areas. This is often justified as a need to focus on high crime areas, and it is hard to prove that the law is not being enforced in wealthier areas. It is generally agreed that law enforcement of drug laws and other crimes without victims is more intense in poor and minority neighborhoods, and that more persons from these areas are incarcerated for these offenses (Annie E. Casey Foundation, 2006a; Western & Wildeman, 2009). One response to this is to decriminalize drug possession and use. There also needs to be a look at the extent to which offenses by persons of higher socio-economic status are handled informally or diverted from court actions. One answer is to have police review boards that deal with unequal law enforcement practices in relation to minorities and low income persons.

Civil Rights

The civil rights movement that began in the 1950s introduced what has been termed the "civil rights era," which started with the passage of the federal Civil Rights Act of 1964 that abolished discrimination in employment for such attributes as color, religion, national origin, and sex. It also abolished discrimination in places of public accommodation, such as restaurants, hotels and theaters. The act also mandated faster integration of schools based on the U.S. Supreme Court decision in *Brown v. Board of Education* that racially segregated schools were not equal. The Civil Rights Act was followed by the Voting Rights Act of 1965, which abolished racial discrimination in voting and empowered federal authorities to intervene at the state level to guarantee them. Subsequent legislation dealt with discrimination in housing, lending and other business activities, and the use of public facilities. The era also saw federal actions followed by similar state and local actions that were extended to include the rights of the disabled, homosexuals, and other populations.

The civil rights movement has always had as its main target the problem of racial discrimination, especially the discrimination against African Americans. The heritage of slavery that deprived

African Americans of virtually all rights has endured, and thus the effectiveness of various policy actions aimed at eliminating this heritage needs to be examined. Racial discrimination mainly stems from difference in physical appearance, especially between African Americans and whites, which has led to a belief of inherent racial superiority that has fed the social dominance needs of many whites. There are several cultural distinctions between darkness and whiteness. Darkness tends to be associated more with evil, decline, decay, and death, as expressed in the term the Dark Ages, and whiteness tends to be associated with light, purity, goodness, and progress. Despite the passage of the Fair Housing Act, some African Americans still face discrimination when trying to purchase homes in predominately white neighborhoods. According to several studies (Thernstrom & Thernstrom, 1997; Massey, 2007), whites have been less likely to buy a home in a neighborhood that was more than 15 percent African American.

Historically, racial superiority was further reinforced by the institution of chattel slavery, which treated African Americans as subhuman items to be bought and sold like animals, without personal freedom and basic human rights. When slavery was ended, there was still almost total segregation of African Americans, especially in areas where they were more prevalent, that included where they could live, where they went to school, and the use of virtually all public facilities. In employment, most African Americans were segregated into low-paying jobs that they had been forced to do as slaves. For males, this included mostly dirty, physically demanding low-skilled jobs and service jobs, such as janitors, groundskeepers, porters and waiters; and for females, the jobs mainly involved being maids and servants. Hence most African Americans had low-incomes and were disproportionately represented among low-income persons in the total population, which adversely affected the support of whites for most social welfare programs. Thus, the feeling of white superiority has such deep roots that it has been an important aspect of the dominant American culture, whether whites will admit it or not. Many whites, for example, see African Americans as having superior physical attributes and inferior intellectual attributes compared to whites (Tatum, 1997).

Racism has been further fostered by the survival of the fittest ethos that, as has been noted, led to a need among whites whose status was threatened to oppress competition from African Americans. At the time of the Civil War, there are records of Irish Americans in New York attacking freed African Americans for taking jobs away from them, by being willing to work for lower wages. Another complication is that the race struggle is enmeshed with the class struggle, as racial minorities are heavily lower class. As has been repeatedly pointed out, equality of opportunity for African Americans threatens lower class whites who fear they will be displaced. This serves to break up the class struggle and also to blame the victim for unemployment.

The civil rights movement also dealt with discrimination directed against people's ethnicity and national origin, but this generally is now less of a problem than racial discrimination. America was largely settled by Europeans: the English, Irish, Germans, Italians, Poles, Scandinavians, and Jews. This gave rise to religious discrimination, primarily against Roman Catholics and Jews. Most European ethnic groups have been well assimilated, and so religious discrimination is less a factor today than it once was. In recent decades, however, discrimination has risen against Hispanics, particularly Puerto Ricans and Mexicans, who have come to the continental United States to do low-paid work in farming, business, industry and many types of service jobs.

Hispanics often face the problem of language barriers and limited education. Hence they need to be included in affirmative action efforts to help them get an education so they will qualify for better jobs, and to give them more employment opportunities. There are also questions about the rights of native peoples, especially American Indians, including whether they have special property rights for land that was taken away from them before the establishment of legal property entitlement. The problem is that they sometimes claim rights for property that has become valuable but that does not seem to be justified. A better approach might be to give them special opportunities to purchase real estate. What seems clearly needed is for Native Americans to be fully integrated and not segregated in special reservations, and that they, like peoples of other nationalities, be free from suffering caused by discrimination.

Enforcement of Civil Rights

Civil rights agencies were established at all levels of government to receive and investigate complaints of discrimination that could be followed up on and remedied in accordance with their orders. It has not been easy to prove discrimination, because it is often difficult to argue that persons were denied a job or housing because of reasons of race, nationality, or sex alone. Some employers set high qualifications based on education and job experience that were intended to rule out African Americans and other minorities. There was some effort by civil rights agencies to rule out high qualifications that had little to do with ability to perform a job. Similarly, the use of tests for employment was questioned and disallowed when the material included in the test had little do with the actual requirements for the job. In housing it was fairly easy for real estate agents to steer Africans Americans and other racial and ethnic minorities away from areas where whites predominated. In some places, testers were used to prove that there was actually a housing vacancy when another tester of a different race or nationality had been turned away on the basis that there were no vacancies.

Initially, discrimination in employment was handled on a case-by-case basis by civil rights agencies and the courts. The problem was that action was slow and time consuming, and it was always possible to argue that those hired were better qualified. There was also a backlash against the civil rights legislation to lessen its enforcement. This led to the use of affirmative action that is designed to increase employment and education opportunities for women and racial and ethnic minorities. Affirmative action is intended to assure that minorities and women are represented at all levels of employment and education where they were previously underrepresented. This emphasis on inclusiveness is more socially acceptable than the emphasis on equality of opportunity, which displaces others in the competition for scare jobs and, as has been pointed out, leads to resistance.

Affirmative action was initially ordered by President Johnson to address problems involving federal employment. The coverage was similar to the Civil Rights Act, including race, color, national origin, religion and sex. Coverage was extended by President Nixon to federal contractors, and has since been adopted by most states and local governments for public employees and public contractors. It has also been extended to education, especially higher education, and seeks to increase enrollment of minorities and women where they are underrepresented, and to focus on enrollment in programs such as engineering, which historically have had few minorities and women.

Federal affirmative action policies require employers to develop plans to increase employment of minorities and women at all levels where they are found to be underutilized in a particular job group, in terms of the expected availability of those who are qualified. Covered employers are expected to make a good faith effort to reduce underutilization. This may include expanded effort at outreach, recruitment, training and other activities. Plans are expected to include establishing goals for hiring and promoting. Goals are targets not only to be reached but against which progress is measured. Enforcement of the orders for federal contracts was assigned to the U.S. Department of Labor Office of Contract Compliance. It requires contractors to engage in self-analysis for the purpose of discovering any barriers to equal employment opportunities, and to make a good faith effort to deal with under-utilization. Where it is found that these requirements are not being met, the Office of Contract Compliance may order that the contract be terminated or suspended. Similar requirement are made by most state and local governments for contractors that they cover.

There is evidence that affirmative action has worked in many places, and numerous employers have discovered that their public image is improved by having more minority and women employees. For example, professional baseball now requires teams to interview at least one minority candidate in filling the position of team manager. Affirmative action has led to the discovery of real talent, such as General Colin Powell, an African American who became Army brigadier general as a result of affirmative action efforts, rose to become chairman of the Joint Chiefs of Staff, and thereafter served as George W. Bush's secretary of state.

Affirmative action programs have been attacked in the courts as furthering reverse discrimination by excluding more qualified applicants. The courts have generally sustained affirmative action when applicants have been within the bounds of those regarded as qualified by employers and colleges and universities. It should be clear that affirmative action does not call for hiring or admitting unqualified persons, which could lead to a backlash against it. It is important to remember that affirmative action determines who gets available jobs or gets admitted to educational institutions and programs. It does not eliminate unemployment, make wages more equal, or increase the overall number of students admitted. Hence, it should not be regarded as a substitute for the class struggle, or the basic struggle for socio-economic rights, but, rather, as a means for getting more socio-economic equality among people of different races, nationalities, religions, and sexes.

The concern about reverse discrimination cannot be taken lightly. Some extremists, in dealing with civil rights, feel that the only real solution is to seek dominance rather than togetherness and inclusiveness, Where possible, they have advocated that new employees, those admitted to certain higher education programs, and those appointed to boards and commissions be predominately African American. More commonly, there has been advocacy for a combination that includes women, African Americans and Hispanics, on the basis that they are predominate in the population, and, hence, more white males should be displaced. This displacement may be justified on the basis that white males are no longer the predominate group in the population or the labor force, and that seems to be a valid goal. It needs to be approached gradually to avoid conflict, however, and there needs to be recognition that white males will rarely accept being disproportionately excluded.

What must be emphasized is that social justice should be based on togetherness, with broad representation of all population groups, and some consideration of their numbers in the applicant or employment pool and in the affected population groups. This discussion leads to concerns about employments that are predominately women, African American, Hispanic or from some other minority group. The predominance of these groups can be viewed as giving them more opportunities for employment, but, in most instances, it represents employing them as a source of low- cost labor (U.S. Census Bureau, 2011).

Results and Challenges

The civil rights era has seen marked progress in lessening discrimination and socio-economic differences by race, national origin, religion, sex, sexual orientation and physical conditions. Hence these groups are found in employments where they had been largely excluded, and the earnings gap between them and the dominant majority has, until recently, been dramatically reduced. There have been more efforts to provide equality of opportunity, especially in education. Another significant development has been the increasing presence of women and minorities in leadership and high status positions in business, government, and social organizations. The success of the civil rights era seems culminated in the election of President Barack Obama as the first African American president, and whose wife, as first lady, is not many generations from slavery. A symbol of this progress in civil rights was the 2010 State of the Union Address, with President Obama standing before Vice President Biden, the first Roman Catholic vice president, and Speaker Nancy Pelosi, the first woman speaker. All of this has only been possible in the last 50 years.

With these developments as a background, the challenge is to consider what policy actions will further progress civil rights, especially in employment and earnings. An important indicator in reducing discrimination in employment is to look at trends in the gap between minorities and women and the dominant white male majority. In 1940, the average African American male earned just 40 percent of that earned by the average white worker. Owing mainly to the movement of African American males from farm jobs in the South to man the war industries during World War II, and the enforcement of civil rights in war contracts, the gap closed to 50 percent in 1950. After the war, the reduction in the gap continued markedly, from 55 percent in 1960 to 76 percent in 1975. Since then, however, the 25 percent gap has persisted (Christie, 2010; Massey, 2007). According to recent figures from the Bureau of Labor Statistics, whites earned a median of $756 weekly during the three months ended June 30, 2010, which was 25 percent more than blacks, who earned $607 (Christie, 2010).

Comparing median family income by race, the African American income was only 54.3 percent of whites in 1950, and by 1970 had increased to 61.3 percent; by 2004, it remained close to that figure, at 62.3 percent in 2004 (See Table 7.1 on the next page, *Median Income by Race and Ethnicity & Percent of White Family Income 1950-2004*). Between 2005 and 2010, however, the median household net worth of African Americans, as well as Hispanics and Asians, fell by roughly 60 percent while the median net worth of white households fell only 23 percent (Luhby, 2012).

The gap in median family income between Hispanics and whites has been somewhat better than that for African Americans. Hispanic median family income as a percent of white family income remained fairly constant at around 64 percent, and in 2008 increased to 72.5 percent (U.S. Census Bureau, 2005, 2011). Dealing with these large gaps in median family income, and the fact that they are not closing further, with its implication for normal child development and family life, presents a special challenge in the struggle for social justice.

Table 7.1

Median Income by Race and Ethnicity &
Percent of White Family Income 1950-2004

			Black Families		Hispanic Families	
		White Families				
	All Families	Median		% of White		% of White
	Median	Median	Median	Family	Median	Family
Year	Income	Income	Income	Income	Income	Income
2004	54, 061	56,700	35,328	62.3	35,401	62.4
2000	55,821	58,416	37,505	64.2	38,450	65.8
1990	49,545	51,734	30,023	58.0	32,837	63.5
1980	45,647	47,560	27,519	57.9	31,953	67.2
1970	41,569	43,123	26,453	61.3		
1960	30,374	31,537	17,457	55.4		
1950	22,055	22,892	12,419	54.3		

Source: U.S. Census Bureau, 2005

The fact that the earnings gap and the rate of unemployment for African Americans has been frozen since the mid 1970s raises questions as to why this has happened and what policy actions are needed to resume progress. One explanation for the failure to close the gap further has been the decline in the number of manufacturing jobs, which primarily has affected the African American males who have been forced to take lower paying service jobs (Schmitt &

Zipperer, 2008). The experience during and after World War II indicates that African Americans benefited most from economic growth, especially in high paying manufacturing jobs. Affirmative action also works best in an expanding economy, when there are new positions to be filled and hence fewer whites will be displaced. Thus one essential factor in closing the gap is to increase economic growth that expands the rate of employment. Also, it is essential to try to slow the outsourcing to other countries of high paying manufacturing jobs.

Another factor that keeps the gap frozen has been the backlash against the civil rights movement marked by oppressive actions to keep African Americans, especially males, out of the socio-economic mainstream. One such action was the increased imprisonment of African American males, primarily for drug offenses. Hence it would be helpful if the possession of various types of drugs were decriminalized as is being done in many progressive European countries. Another factor was oppressive welfare cuts that increasingly cut off the able-bodied unemployed, disproportionately affecting African Americans. Here it seems essential to put more of the unemployed, especially unemployed youth, to work in work for relief programs, as discussed in Chapter 3 (especially the section on policies dealing with unemployment). As African Americans are disproportionately represented among those with low incomes, any redistribution of income through social welfare programs will importantly help African Americans.

These policy actions for African Americans deal more with the consequences of lower earnings than with their causes. The research data cited indicates that there is still real racial discrimination in employment, and that when controlled for such variables as education, veteran and marital status, region, urban residence, number of children, and hours worked, a significant racial gap of 20 percent persists (Massey, 2007).

As regards unemployment when compared to whites, the rate of unemployment of African Americans is about twice as high

(U.S. Bureau of Labor Statistics, 2011c). Numerous studies that use testers of different races but with similar qualifications have found that there is still considerable discrimination by race that applies to various levels of skills, and that education and training by themselves will not eliminate discrimination in the employment of African Americans (Annie E. Casey Foundation, 2006b).

Lack of education is frequently used to blame the victim, especially African Americans, for unemployment and low wage jobs, as previously discussed. Since the data indicate that high school graduation has little effect on the employment opportunities of African Americans, it is clear that their economic circumstances must not be blamed on their failure to graduate from high school. Therefore other policy actions, such as stepping up affirmative action, needs to be tried.

Much discrimination towards African Americans in employment has its roots in slavery. Slavery established a cultural view that African Americans are a source of low-paid labor, and are to be valued for their physical rather than for their mental abilities. Hence, much of their employment to this day is in low-paying jobs that require physical strength.

The best policy actions to change this attitude towards the employment of African Americans would seem to be actions that give them more equality of opportunity in education, so that they can qualify for more types of employment, and then make more vigorous use of affirmative action to see that they are hired. Affirmative action must not just focus on getting African Americans hired, but also on their promotion to higher level positions. This should be a key factor in closing the earnings gap. Attitudes are most readily changed when they are supported by experience. When, as a result of affirmative action, African Americans demonstrate they can fill intellectually demanding jobs, this changes attitudes and encourages the hiring of more qualified African Americans—just as the election of President Obama, who demonstrates considerable intellect, has been a factor in changing attitudes towards African Americans.

The fact that the earnings gap is much wider for median family income probably reflects the reality that more white families have two earners whereas many African American families have a single female head of household (Thernstrom & Thernstrom, 1997; Simms, Fortuny, & Henderson, 2009). Family structure has been found to impact differences in employment and income. Only 18 percent of African American families are in married-family households, whereas 42 percent of white families are in married-family households. The lack of a two-parent household may make it difficult to balance responsibilities in the home with the need to work (Simms, et al., 2009). Again, slavery did little to establish males as the breadwinners, as they received no pay. When slavery was abolished, most African American males were not hired for jobs that paid enough to support a family in the style of whites, and hence they were humiliated when they tried. Affirmative action, if it leads to better paying, more secure jobs, could aid marriage. Also, social welfare programs that would help the disadvantaged in family formation would help, especially with providing affordable housing, such as through rent subsidies tied to specific housing units, and with mortgage costs for first- time home buyers.

Many African American males also were raised in homes without fathers, and thus did not have fathers as role models or as sources of support while developing a male identity (Pitts, 2006). Having more male mentors and teachers to serve as educated role models could help many African American males. There also needs to be more mutual support groups, sponsored by churches and social service agencies, for African American males.

The civil rights movement combined with the women's movement in efforts to eliminate discrimination against women, and to give them more opportunities for employment and social participation. All societies have made distinctions in sex roles that have become a major part of their cultural tradition. Mostly women have been restricted to the domestic roles of raising children and household chores, while men have been given the main role of working outside the home to provide the family with needed resources. They also have been assigned the more physically demanding tasks, including protecting the women and children in the event of war and from crime and other hostile forces. The result is that, in most societies, males have been treated as dominant and women as subservient. Rapidly changing technology has brought about major changes in sex roles. Birth control and other factors have led to a declining birth rate, and an increased number of women participate in the workforce (Cohn & Livingston, 2010; Sullivan, 2009).

The use of machinery that requires less physical strength made the employment of more women possible. An example was the development of the automatic starter, which enabled women to drive without using the physically demanding crank. Most significant was giving women the right to vote and full citizenship, which has increased their political power. That factor, combined with the changing roles of women, has led to successful efforts to include women in most jobs. Also more women have been selected and elected for leadership positions in business and government.

The dynamics of dealing with discrimination based on sex is markedly different than that of race, which involves dealing with a culture of belief in white inherent racial superiority. As women, like men, are spread among all social classes, socio-economic status is less of a factor in eliminating discrimination by sex than it is by race, especially for African Americans. As women represent the majority of voters, there can be less consideration of social class factors. In fact, it seems that some women political candidates have a special appeal to politically independent women voters, where they can give the impression of being moderate politically but concerned with other issues important to women. Women are also helped by not being overly represented among the disadvantaged, giving them more opportunity to benefit from education, especially higher education. That leads to employment in higher paying, more secure jobs. Hence, as a result of the combination of the civil rights movement and the women's movement, there has been substantial progress in eliminating discrimination against women. There have been successful efforts to include women in many jobs where they historically have been largely excluded, such as law enforcement, the military, and business administration, and in many professional roles traditionally dominated by men: lawyers, physicians, engineers, and the clergy, among others. Many social organizations that were exclusively male now admit women so that, for example, there are few exclusively male universities and colleges, and many that were traditionally male now have admitted more women than men.

What has been especially notable is the number of women in leadership positions in occupations that had been exclusively male, with the result that the so-called glass ceiling is disappearing. One is impressed by the obvious growth of the number of women in leadership positions in politics, government, business and industry, including the highly prestigious finance and banking industry that had been almost exclusively male. Prominent examples of such women include Secretary of State Hillary Rodham Clinton, in the Barack Obama administration; Secretary of State Condoleezza Rice, in the George W. Bush administration; Carly Fiorina, former head of Hewlett Packard; and Marissa Mayer, the current head of Yahoo, to name only a few.

It took the traditional U.S. Episcopal Church only about 30 years after ordaining women to have a woman as head bishop (Brown, 2010). Despite this progress, there are still many higher status and more lucrative occupations denominated by men than women. For example in 2009, women who were employed full-time on a wage salary earned on average 20 percent less than men (See Table 7.2 *Median usual weekly earnings of full-time wage and salary workers 1979-2009*). There are countless examples, such as male doctors and dentists in offices with female nurses and assistants; male pilots and female stewardesses; and male corporate bosses and female secretaries.

Table 7.2
Median Usual Weekly Earnings of Full-time Wage and Salary Workers 1979-2009

Year	Total Men	Total Women	Women's Earnings as a % of Men's
1979	$292	$182	62.3
1980	$313	$201	64.2
1990	$481	$346	71.9
2000	$641	$493	76.9
2009	$819	$657	80.2

Source: Solis & Hall, 2010

There are occupations that, by their nature, will probably be dominated by one sex or the other. Women probably will be found more in occupations concerned with the care and teaching of young children and in nursing, while men will continue to be found more in physically demanding jobs in construction and in baggage and freight handling. The task is not only to use affirmative action to get more women into positions—especially high status ones—that have been predominately male, but to increase the level of pay for predominately female positions. The federal Fair Pay Act requires employers to pay women the same as men for similar jobs, but this does not apply across employments. Here, union organizing may be most successful, as it certainly has been rewarding for teachers, nurses and airline stewardesses.

Future Efforts to Deal with Discrimination

Despite these actions, further progress by both race and sex will not be easy, especially as it deals with the residual elements that will be hard to eliminate. The best hope seems to be to put in-

182

creasing efforts into affirmative action. The actions in the Obama administration of including more African Americans, Hispanics and women in top level positions has set a climate for more vigorous affirmative action efforts. In regard to public policies to promote affirmative action, the federal government requires that all federal agencies have affirmative action plans, and that this practice must be extended to those organizations that have government contracts. This includes about 22 percent of the work force (Walsh, 2010). Most state and local governments have similar requirements, but the combination of federal, state and local affirmative action plans probably cover less than half the labor force. It would seem that affirmative action requirements should be extended to all employers with 25 or more employees, with some sort of sanctions, such as fines, imposed on those who do not comply and make a good faith effort. For employers engaged in interstate commerce, it could be a federal requirement.

The organization of affirmative action implementation needs to be considered. One problem is that enforcement of affirmative action in employment seems split between the federal, state or local contracting agency with which there is a contract and labor departments and civil rights agencies that have responsibility for the overall administration of affirmative action. Enforcement between the public contracting agencies and the contractors seems to depend on the relationship between these organizations and, hence, tends to be haphazard. It would seem, therefore, that if affirmative action is to be strengthened, there needs to be a comprehensive affirmative action strategy of identifying where action is most needed in terms of employment and education.

This should be done on the national level for employment and education agencies that are covered by national requirements, and similarly on the state and local levels for those who are covered by them. In order to accomplish this, it would seem indicated that federal, state, and local civil rights agencies be given full authority to develop and coordinate the implementation of a comprehensive plan. Coordination would involve working with labor departments and government personnel departments in dealing with affirmative action in employments, and also with departments of education and higher education for affirmative action in education. Local poverty agencies could also be involved in providing job training, childcare and transportation when this is needed. As part of the plan there might be staff in employment agencies that would give special help to racial and ethnic minorities and women, so that their needs could be considered as part of affirmative action. Also, all public and private organizations that are covered by affirmative action requirements should be required to appoint an executive officer charged with responsibility for developing and implementing the organization's affirmative action plan in compliance with the requirements.

Chapter 8
The Politics of Policy Actions

The struggle for social justice largely involves the struggle between laissez-faire conservatives and social liberals that takes place within the context of the class struggle, and that mostly involves public policy concerns that occur in the political arena. In considering the political factors in enacting public policies to further social justice objectives, it is well to examine forces that have shaped the politics of public policy action in recent years. The Great Depression of the 1930s upset the status quo and resulted in both a depressed middle class and a new environment for governmental intervention. The Roosevelt administration, through its New Deal, made it possible to set a liberal agenda, which lasted for almost 40 years. The significant milestones of this period have been noted, including labor legislation such as the Wagner Act, which protected the right of workers to organize into trade unions and facilitated large expansions of the labor movement—a source of substantial support for liberal policies. The New Deal period also produced legislation that initiated federal social welfare programs in the areas of social insurance and public assistance, as well as programs that provided nutrition, housing and health services to meet the needs of the depressed middle class.

Another significant development was the use of federal fiscal policies involving tax cuts and deficit financing to promote full employment and economic growth, which has been called "expansionist" economics. This has been supported by most economists using macro-economic analysis. Though there is often heated debate about how to bring down the deficit and stimulate the economy between liberals and conservatives, the main debate is on how much emphasis to give to public expenditures, which the liberals prefer, or to tax cuts, which the conservatives prefer.

World War II ended the period of high unemployment and created a demand for labor. The relatively full employment of the postwar years made it possible to pass the federal Civil Rights Act, which abolished discrimination in employment by race, nationality, religion and sex, as these groups could be hired without displacing too many other employees in an expanding economy. Also, the increased affluence of African Americans and their increasing educational attainment enabled them to take more independent action under strong leaders, such as Martin Luther King. This created a climate that enabled the civil rights movement to push for legislation to abolish other forms of discrimination, most notably in voting by the enactment of the federal Voting Rights Act, and also for dealing with discrimination in financial services, housing, and human rights, especially for groups such as the disabled, gays and lesbians, and women. It also established an ongoing effort to integrate public schools by race.

The progress in liberal legislation began to unravel during the 1970s, culminating in the election of President Reagan and the ascendancy of conservatism. The latter was caused in part by a rise in inflation and a slowdown in economic growth. They resulted in less support for the concepts of expansionist economics based on increasing demand for goods and services, which was supposed to result in growth with very modest inflation. Expansionist economics was replaced by the ascendancy of what is called austerity economics, which blamed the lack of economic growth on a shortage of investment capital that public and private growth in consumption had crowded out. The concept of supply-side economics was introduced, which blamed business taxes and personal income taxes as destroying the incentive to invest. This provided a rationale for public expenditures for social welfare to be constrained and for taxes on corporations and the wealthy to be lowered. Also, it was advocated that social insurances such as Social Security

186

should be replaced by individual savings accounts that would provide more funds for investment and lower taxes for benefits. Liberal economists rejected the ideas that expansionist economics had failed, pointing out that inflation was created by what was called the oil shock of rapidly rising oil prices that ended when oil prices declined. They also pointed out that the Reagan administration practiced expansionist policies by increasing defense expenditures financed by raising the federal debt.

Another big factor in bringing about the conservative revolution was a backlash against the civil rights movement by those threatened with increasing competition from minorities and women for good jobs, which were becoming scarcer due to the decline in economic growth. This was particularly threatening to lower-class whites who had moved their families to suburbia (a symbol of having "made it") and into the middle class, and placed their children in schools with upper-class children. However, the increased housing cost strained their budgets and the last thing they wanted was increased competition from African Americans and other minorities who were also moving into the suburbs. The result was a shift of support to the conservatives as a means of curtailing the civil rights movement. Reagan got about two-thirds of the white male vote.

In the South, federal voting rights legislation stopped the whites-only primaries that kept the African Americans out of Democratic Party primaries, which produced one party states. When the Voting Rights Act allowed African Americans to participate in primaries, the white response was to shift to the conservative Republican Party and make it a party of the whites. This cut across the class struggle and resulted in lower-class whites aligning themselves with the party of the wealthy. As a result, the class struggle for greater economic equality and security was replaced by conservative causes that appealed to low-income whites, one of which was an emphasis on social control to deal with crime and deviancy. This was facilitated by increased media coverage of youth violence, and rising fear of the growing menace of the drug problem. As has been noted, conservatives were able to increase white solidarity across class lines by oppressive measures that were clearly targeted to African Americans. One was "welfare reform" that especially deprived African American children and their families of basic necessities. The "reforms" were justified as discouraging out-of-wedlock births, chronic unemployment, and dependency on welfare. Also drug laws were more strongly enforced for African Americans, who were labeled as the main source of the problem (Western & Wildeman, 2009).

Other sources of increasing fear and confusion were changes in family life and the growing complexity of modern life that conservatives have been able to exploit. Changes in family life have been especially upsetting for many, as more couples live together outside of marriage along with increased rates of out-of-wedlock births and divorce. Many have been especially threatened by increased use of abortion and greater acceptance of homosexuality. Social conservatives have readily embraced preservation of traditional family values and the Protestant ethic and opposed both abortion and homosexuality, which has become one of the main bases of their political support.

The increasing complexity of the global economy has also left many confused and fearful. Few can understand the complexities of the political economy, such as the relationship of taxes, interest rates, the national debt, balance of payments, low wages, and unemployment to the economy. This leads to uncertainty as to what policies are in their self-interest. There is also the perception that big government is in the hands of special interests that have little concern about the general welfare. All of this leads to a fear of change that has helped conservatives to sell the idea of retaining the status quo and returning to the good old days of the private market system with minimum governmental control and low taxes. This was well illustrated in the defeat of the Clinton health care reform efforts that, for many, were too complex with too much change.

Much of this shift to conservatism would not have happened if the labor movement had remained strong and the liberal political parties could have relied on the union vote. Unions can especially help members understand what public policies are in their self-interest and provide solidarity in backing them. As was noted, unions worldwide have been hurt by what is called the post- industrial age, which has been characterized by a loss of industrial jobs and an increase in service jobs that are not as easy to unionize. One result has been that, throughout the world, liberal parties have had to move more to the center. The strength of unions is based on numbers and solidarity. Where most workers are unionized, it is easy for them to walk off the job or refuse to deliver supplies when nonunion workers are hired. When there are fewer union members, it is easier to contract out jobs to nonunion workers. Generally, businesses seek out low-wage and low-cost areas in expanding their operations, and are attracted to places where unions are already weaker, such as in the South.

The election of a Democrat, Bill Clinton, as president in 1992 did little to counter the conservative trend. His efforts for universal health care failed to pass the Congress and led to election of a Republican Congress in 1994. Then Congress managed to turn Clinton's welfare reform proposal into one of the most oppressive actions against poor children and their families ever passed. The Clinton administration did manage to increase the income tax on the wealthy and lower unemployment, but the inequalities in the distribution of income changed little. Whatever gains in the name of social justice that were made during the Clinton years were mostly undone by the eight years of the Bush administration, which reduced taxes for the wealthy and businesses and further increased inequality of income. It even made an unsuccessful effort to begin to dismantle the welfare state by beginning privatization of retirement benefits under Social Security. It did privatize drug

189

coverage for the elderly rather than include it under Medicare. It cut back on low income housing programs and made an effort to aid churches directly for social service programs that would have used charity as a substitute for social justice.

The election of President Obama gave hope that the conservative dominance had come to an end. The Obama administration was able to enact the health care reform legislation that previous Democratic administrations had not succeeded in enacting. It also enacted economic stimulus legislation that provided federal funds to aid the unemployed and for social welfare, schools, roads and highways, and energy projects. It bailed out banks and businesses that were regarded as "too big to fail" and enacted legislation for more regulation of financial services, including establishing the Consumer Financial Protection Bureau as an independent agency. All of these public policy actions were strongly backed by social liberals with virtually no help from Republicans.

However, the Republicans were able to pull out all the stops of their power in the 2010 midterm elections and recapture enough independent voters who had voted for Obama to gain control of the House of Representatives, additional seats in the U.S. senate, and control of many state legislatures and governorships. The Republicans were able to use their vast financial resources and control of much of the press to take advantage of the increasing level of unemployment, by claiming it indicate the economic stimulus had not worked. They also claimed the health reform legislation would increase unemployment. Both of these claims were highly questionable, but they went largely uncontested in the media. The Republicans essentially got away with charging that health care reform increased unemployment, when it was estimated that 32 million more people would get health insurance coverage, and that this, in turn, would result in the increased employment of thousands of health workers. The conservatives turned to their usual themes of the danger of big government and the need to reduce public expenditures and balance the budget, without any reference to what this would do to unemployment. They dismissed the government bailout of failing businesses regarded as too big to fail as unnecessary, and only a temporary emergency measure. All of this showed how deep the roots of conservatism are, and that the nation is far from moving to the left. At this juncture, it is hard to predict what lies ahead. Probably there will be some changes to the health care reform bill, and it is possible that it will be reduced to just a block grant to the states to help with their health care costs.

Political Strategies

Politics has been defined as the art of the possible. Hence, the task is to find political strategies that will make some policy actions possible. Previous chapters have dealt with what seem to be politically possible actions, but in devising policy strategies it is important that they be conceptualized. It would seem that such strategies could be conceptualized into two groups. One is to use the political appeal of what can be called populism, which seeks to unite the common people around their social and economic self-interests. The other is to use the political appeal of what is called the work ethic. Populism largely involves the class struggle, i.e., between the very rich and powerful and the rest of the population, but seeks to broaden it by appealing to more than just the working class, which still has to be its main constituency. Populism can be furthered by the provision of more universal social welfare services that provide benefits for all regardless of need, such as social insurance benefits provided for retirement, disability benefits, unemployment benefits, health care benefits, and paid sick leave.

Populism can also be served by the use of subsidies and tax credits that are universal, and that provide help with the increasing costs of housing, medical care and higher education. The use of tax credits such as the Earned Income Tax Credit (EITC) has been politically popular because it provides a tax credit only for workers; and the tax credit could be used as a way to provide affordable medical insurance and housing costs. There should be more support for means-tested programs when they are attached to universal services, as evidenced by the general support for supplementary security income (SSI) for the aged and disabled, who do not receive sufficient Social Security benefits or who have not been eligible for them in the first place. As was mentioned, means-tested benefits could be extended to those who have used up the unemployment benefits.

Another populist strategy is to promote human rights for all, especially the Universal Declaration of Human Rights. The provision of human rights is the foundation on which the struggle for social justice is based. Here, particular attention needs to be paid to economic rights to basic essentials such as food, clothing, housing and medical care; the right to a job at decent wages; to social security; to unemployment benefits; and the right to organize trade unions. All of these have been eroded as conservatives have gained political power. There must be a readiness to call the deprivation of human rights outright oppression and more willingness to confront conservatives for using politics for human oppression. Service workers need to be more aware of when they are being used as what may be called "mystifiers," when oppressors use token gestures such as soup kitchens, food baskets and Christmas toys to convince the oppressed that they are really caring people. Hopefully an awareness of human rights may activate compassionate concerns in many conservative-leaning persons who will see this as the foundation of a more humane world. The emphasis on human rights may also counter some of the morality of blaming the victim for unemployment and the use of punitive social welfare cuts.

The work ethic has been the main ideological basis for laissez-faire conservatives. The ethic states that all able-bodied persons should seek employment in the labor market that pays people a just wage according to their skill and how much their employment contributes to value-added to the goods and services they provide.

Thus, individuals are regarded as masters of their socio-economic circumstances, in that they will be justly rewarded for the skills they acquire and the effective efforts they make in a survival of the fittest competition. However, this ethos requires that employment opportunities exist. Macro-economic analysis has convinced most economists that employment depends on the aggregate demand for goods and services, and not because workers refuse to work for low wages or that increased supply of highly skilled workers creates demand. It is also obvious that increased unemployment is due to the decline in the functioning of the economy, and not a result of workers having less skill or making less effort to find work.

Hence, laissez-faire conservatives have had to accept some economic stimulus so that the main debate is how much to cut taxes or increase expenditures and how large a deficit to incur. Populism can embrace the notion of economic stimulus and put emphasis on using unemployment insurance to keep up demand and reduce the downward economic spiral. The problem of paying workers benefits that are not in exchange for working is somewhat countered by using the payroll tax, so that workers' earnings are put in a special fund out of which benefits are paid. The work ethic also calls for security when a person is no longer able to work due to illnesses and disability or wants to retire. Retirement is best provided by Social Security benefits that are paid for by the payroll tax. As was suggested, unemployment insurance could be extended to cover paid sick leave that might be used when employer paid sick leave benefits run out. Clearly, employer-paid sick leave benefits, if required, must have a time limit if they are to be affordable to employers. Benefits should be paid after time limits have been used up, and social insurance is an effective solution.

Other forms of insurance, such as health insurance, can be sold for their economic stimulus effect, especially as the health sector is becoming a larger portion of the economy and the source of many jobs, particularly for minority women. The construction of needed, affordable housing is another means of stimulating the economy, as most periods of economic recession have been marked by a decline in construction. Another use of the work ethic that has been suggested is to put the long-term unemployed, especially unemployed youth, to work through public works projects, work relief or work-for-relief programs.

Organizing Support for Political Action

A major task in building political support for public policies to further social justice is through community organizing, to involve individuals and organizations in a joint effort for policy actions. Community organizing could involve setting a climate for political action and actively taking a stand in dealing with legislation, endorsing candidates for public office, and contributing time and money to political campaigns. Methods for doing this include studying community conditions and the effectiveness of current policies in meeting needs, such as regards the number of families who lack private health insurance; and publishing reports and issuing press releases to point out the problem and suggest needed policy actions. Action in support of legislation involves issuing alerts to contact legislators and other elected officials by mail, e-mail and phone calls, and taking joint action by signing petitions, holding meetings and conferences and staging rallies. Lobbyists can be used to contact key legislators and in organizing support.

What has been stressed here is the need to look at social justice concerns comprehensively, so that the pieces fit together and the most helpful policy actions are taken. This calls for using community organizations that look at the task comprehensively and can devise a strategy for coordinating the efforts of other more specialized organizations, including forming needed coalitions. On the national level, this would call for increased influence by organizations mainly focused on the ideology of social liberalism and human rights, such as the Brookings Institution and the Center for Budget and Policy Priorities, which focus on studying human needs and recommending comprehensive policy actions. There are other organizations that focus more comprehensively on policy actions, such as Americans for Democratic Action. Also, in order to have more direct government involvement, it is helpful to have government-sponsored commissions at the national, state and local level, with a comprehensive mandate such as a commission on human rights or human services to study where policies need to be strengthened and make recommendations for action. On the state level, there are often private advocacy agencies called by such names as association for human services or councils of social service agencies that are fairly comprehensive. On the local level, there are often community councils or human service organizations for advocacy and coalition building. Ideally these organizations should broadly represent the community population groups.

Another way to engage citizens is to have neighborhood organizations that look comprehensively at neighborhood needs. Neighborhood organizations stem from the settlement house movement developed in the nineteenth century, mostly to serve neighborhoods with large, low-income and immigrant populations. The settlement houses operated programs to help these groups settle in America. They operated classes and work-training programs, health clinics, childcare, and support groups for parents and other social services that provided support. They also took action to improve neighborhood schools, health services, law enforcement, and affordable housing. Neighborhood organizing became an important part of the federal government's poverty program of the 1960s, which was seen as helping the poor pull themselves up by their own bootstraps and taking collective action to improve neighborhood services. These organizations received federal funds that they managed, which were used for job training, employment programs and needed social services, such as childcare and information and referral services. These organizations also sought to be involved in neighborhood development that included low-income housing.

With the end of the poverty program, many of these neighborhood organizations went out of business, but some have continued, financed by state and local governments and by grants from foundations and other fund raising efforts. Many feel that neighborhood advocacy agencies promote togetherness and help neighborhoods feel empowered to improve their conditions. One reason given for support of neighborhood organizations is that they would reduce crime and delinquency. That was based on opportunity theory, which holds that delinquency is the result of feelings of powerlessness and that with opportunity for jobs and a better life the disadvantaged will be more a part of society and have less need to resort to deviancy. Neighborhood organizations need to come together in coalitions for action on state and local legislation that would benefit them.

There are also community organization activities that are more specialized in areas such as education, community development, housing, health and disability services, family and children's services and civil rights and civil liberties. These more specialized organizations are needed so that there can be a more concentrated effort to deal with particular needs that require mobilizing the efforts of those organizations that are involved in these specialized policy concerns. This is especially true in dealing with housing needs, which require community organizations concerned with physical planning and zoning, banking and finance, real estate, and construction, and that involve working with specialized government agencies and legislative committees. Many state and local governments have established commissions in specialized areas, such as those concerned with economic development, women, the aged, children, and various minority groups. They have the legitimacy of public sponsorship and can study needs and make recommendations for policy development. There is a concern about government-sponsored advocacy. These organizations are constrained by the political climate of the times. When there is a need to curtail government expenditure, there are often efforts to restrict their activities or even eliminate them. Comprehensive community organizing activities need to reach out to these specialized organizations to coordinate their work as a part of comprehensive actions.

In organizing to help bring about policy changes for social justice, it is important to reach out and involve organizations in various systems. For example, with the educational system, most teachers and other education organizations would tend to be supportive of efforts for racial integration of schools, equal opportunity for disadvantaged students, and programs for the disabled. Teachers would be especially supportive of programs that do not blame them for the lack of educational progress of the disadvantaged. Parent organizations would vary in their support of these efforts according to their perceived interests. For example, many who fear increased competition of minorities would oppose integration of schools. In dealing with higher education, colleges and universities and their faculties would be supportive of courses dealing with human rights, and for affirmative action programs to serve more minorities and women. Housing programs involve many interests. Real estate agents and banks would be supportive of programs to aid in home ownership, such as tax credits. Those concerned with economic development and the construction industry and its workers would be supportive of the development of affordable housing.

There is often considerable opposition to the development of low-income housing by those who want to exclude low-income families, especially racial and ethnic minorities. Dealing with this opposition often requires the organization of community-sponsored, nonprofit housing agencies that seek to develop affordable housing, especially for low-income families. Here is it generally helpful if faith-based groups that want to help low-income people can sponsor or strongly support these agencies. There is also a need for housing organizations to advocate for the right of families and special need populations to affordable housing that might involve active support of high density zoning, rental assistance, and the rehabilitation and construction of affordable housing.

As medical care becomes a larger share of the economy, many interests are involved, including the providers of health care services, the insurance industry, consumers, and employers who want a healthy labor force. Providers, including health care facilities and their employees—health care professionals, para-professionals and other staff—would generally be supportive of universal health care and third party payments by public and private insurance programs, since with increasing costs these are the main ways health care can be funded. The 2010 health care reform legislation had the support of the American Hospital Association and the American Medical Association. Many professions involved in health care with various specialties want to have their services qualify for third party payments. This has contributed to what many feel is an over-specialization of health care, such as requiring podiatrists to cut toe nails and speech specialists to deal with swallowing problems.

The private insurance industry benefits from the increasing costs of medical care that requires most families to have health insurance to provide protection for health care costs. They, of course, are opposed to a government-run single payer system as is found in most countries with universal health care programs. Thus, private, for-profit health insurers, in order to survive, join all those interests that support laissez-faire conservatives who want this type of insurance that is provided by the market system. In this system, competition would control costs and consumers would have to decide for themselves how much they can afford to spend for health care insurance. Conservatives would limit government policies to subsidizing the health care costs of the poor who clearly do not have the income to pay for even basic health care insurance. Thus, government-supported universal health care has led to a battle between the social liberals and laissez-faire conservatives. The debate over health care reform was won by the liberals in 2010 with the passage of the Affordable Care Act, which was held to be constitutional for the most part by the U.S. Supreme Court in 2012. It is expected to be repealed to some extent, however, by the conservatives, who in 2010 gained control of the Federal House of Representatives, and are continually seeking to increase their numbers and influence in Congress. A better bill, perhaps, could have been passed if the private insurance industry had been included, by providing a universal tax credit for private health insurance. This would have benefited more than those covered by the health care reform bill that was passed and hence more widely supported. The tax credit also would be funded by an increase in the income tax, which would be more redistributive and subject to public regulation to control costs. Here, again, there is a need for special advocacy organizations, such as Families USA, to support policies for the development of health care services that are affordable for all.

Support of Religious Groups

Reaching out for support from religious organizations represents even more of a challenge. Religious organizations establish an ethical base for social justice, as most use some form of the reciprocity ethic of "do unto others as you want others to do unto you," which is usually expressed in terms of love for one's neighbor. Social justice has been called the corporate expression of love for one's neighbor. However, religious organizations get into conflict when moving from the general love of one's neighbor ethic to specific policy actions. The problem is that religious organizations depend on community support that is affected by socio-economic factors. One major factor is the class struggle and the extent to which communities are predominately upper and middle class or lower class. Mainstream Protestant churches, such as Episcopalians, Presbyterians, Lutherans, the United Church of Christ, and Methodists, are predominately middle and upper class (Pew Research Center, 2008). Hence, they are not easily engaged in working-class concerns about employment, wages and unionization. In dealing with social welfare they are often reluctant to support the redistribution of income for entitlements and other programs, as they do not want their income and property taxes increased to fund them. Rarely will these churches support tax increases. In this connection, one can remember wearing a button at a church convention that read "Compassion Before Tax Cuts."

Many churches resort to token efforts to aid the poor, such as food baskets and soup kitchens, that are more symbolic than substantive; and they need to be reminded that charity does not substitute for justice. Christian churches need to be exposed to the teaching of the social gospel that calls for involvement in changing the social order to promote social justice. One way to change the social order is to put more emphasis on human rights, especially the right to a decent, more equal standard of living. Just as churches support the human right that no one should go hungry, they should also support the right that all humans have to belong to a trade union. The more secure and educated middle and upper class church members may respond to human rights that address the right to adequate nutrition, affordable medical care and affordable housing. Due to the resistance of many to low-income housing, with its racial overtones, there is a challenge to religious organizations in the name of human rights to support and sponsor the development of low- and moderate-income housing and other programs for low-income families.

Advocates of social justice working in religious organizations need to constantly reiterate that their mission is to comfort the afflicted and afflict the comfortable, and that rights involve obligations such as progressive income taxes based on ability to pay. Hence, rather than deal with more social class concerns about employment, wages and labor relations, religious organizations could direct their efforts to the provision of human rights. However, it is well to note that some activist church groups have been concerned about low-paid farm labor, sweatshops and child labor. Many middle class churches in urban locations are finding themselves more and more surrounded by low-income people and are trying to reach out to them, which should pull them towards being more politically supportive of social justice issues. They especially have to become more involved in dealing with the need for medical care, housing and social services such as childcare. Urban places of worship should also become more aware of the importance of trade unions in dealing with the needs of low-income people. The Roman Catholic Church, which serves many working-class persons, has been more supportive of the labor movement and public programs to support social justice; but as it became more middle class, its support has lessened in recent years.

Many middle- and upper-class churches and temples perhaps are better suited to dealing with racial and minority rights rather than with social class concerns, as they are more secure and less threatened by competition from minority groups. Hence they can be more supportive of equality of opportunity for racial and other minority groups, which could include racial integration of schools. They could also be supportive of affirmative action policies for more inclusion of qualified minorities. Another interesting development is for religious organizations to sponsor social action efforts that are inter-racial and bring together suburban and central city religious organizations, which can lead to more support for legislation and programs that serve the needs of central city minorities.

Many conservative religious organizations argue that the separation of church and state means that the church should not be involved in advocating for public policies; but religions have always been involved in social reform, as exemplified historically by their actions in the abolition of slavery and in prohibiting the sale of alcoholic beverages. The so-called Christian Right, which is mainly composed of evangelicals, embraces the Protestant ethic of hard work and abstinence, and believes in justice in the labor market that rewards those who work hard and acquire needed skills. Thus, they believe that everyone is responsible for their own welfare and must strive to be self-sufficient. The Protestant ethic supports the values of the laissez-faire conservatives, and its adherents, rather than promote working for social reform, mainly focus on the control of social deviancy, especially in the use of drugs and alcohol. The Christian Right also supports the traditional nuclear family, and is especially opposed to any sexual activities outside of marriage or that involve homosexuality. One of its strengths is that it provides members with a simplistic and definite ethical guidance that mainly deals with what they are against.

Support from Businesses

In general, business organizations favor laissez-faire conservatism that seeks control of labor costs and reduced taxes. Some businesses, using macro-economics, can see the value of a well- paid and economically secure labor force that has money to spend and the confidence as to when to spend it. Henry Ford advocated for a well-paid labor force almost a century ago, as he acknowledged that giving workers more money to spend would foster economic growth. In regard to employee benefits and business taxes for social welfare programs, employers need to see that these expenditures can benefit the economy. Auto companies, for example, need to notice their products in employee parking lots of health care facilities, which their employee health benefits premiums helped to pay for. They also need to see what the Japanese have demonstrated: Employee security through such things as seniority lead to high morale and more productivity. Businesses have also seen the need for good educational institutions, all the way through college and professional school, in developing employees with general know-how, technical skills, proficiency in management and marketing.

There are thousands of political action committees and activities organized by individual businesses and business associations that lobby for various policy actions and engage in various election activities. Often their interests put them at odds with each other, but they generally unite in wanting relief from both business and individual income taxes, and it is here where the struggle between people of different socio-economic classes is mostly fought. Special business and professional interests are a real force in political actions that influence public policies dealing with social justice concerns. As was pointed out, businesses are supportive of in-kind social welfare programs where they are the suppliers of such things as food, housing and medical care. Businesses support both tax subsidies, such as subsidizing home ownership through mortgage interest tax deductions (which are strongly backed by the real estate industry) and tax credits for contributing to employee medical insurance and hiring the unemployed.

Support from Citizen Groups

A big challenge is organizing and seeking support from people's movements as an effective force in shaping public policy decisions. Their main source of power is in collective action they can take as workers, consumers, and voters. It is here where the struggle for social justice is best defined in terms of the needs of the working and middle classes, which have the strength of numbers to be organized for social movements, policy advocacy and election campaigns. The greatest impact will be made if a large number of people from a variety of population groups are involved. The task is to organize populations that have a common special interest in social concerns. One of the strongest people's movements has been the trade union movement. It has not only been a force in bargaining for wages and job security, but is the main force in the struggle between different socio-economic classes, and has been a source for political action to influence public policies.

Union actions in endorsements and in organizing support for candidates are a major factor in election politics. Union advocacy was one of the main forces in support of the New Deal legislation of the Roosevelt administration, and also in passing the Medicare and Medicaid amendments in the 1960s. Hence, there needs to be support for the right of workers to organize and engage in collective bargaining. In support of unions, economic policies need to strengthen domestic growth in manufacturing and curtail the outsourcing of high-wage manufacturing jobs that are unionized. The decline in union membership throughout the world has fostered a shift towards conservatism.

Another population group that has been organized effectively is the aged, where there is a common concern for economic security and medical care. The AARP (formerly American Association of Retired Persons) has been a real force in legislative advocacy, with a large national membership, chapters in most metropolitan areas, and publications that deal with public policy issues. Another organized population is the women's movement. The women's vote has become a distinctive factor in the political process. The movement's main activity has been in advocating for women's civil rights, increased educational and training opportunities, and pay equity with men. Women transcend class lines, and the women's movement has been more inclined to work for equality of opportunity than equality of condition. Nonetheless, women tend to be more supportive than men of social welfare programs for economic security, housing and medical care.

Racial and ethnic groups that are mainly from the lower classes have historically been interested in social justice concerns, and have been organized for political action. African American organizations, such as the National Association for the Advancement of Colored People (NAACP) and the Urban League, have had as their main objective public policies for civil rights, equal opportunities and ending racial discrimination. African American politicians, however, have generally tried to build support using the class struggle, because that is where the votes are. Ethnic groups such as Hispanics, Italians, Poles, and Asians have formal and informal groups that are involved in policy actions. These groups need to broaden their advocacy to involve individuals of other ethnicities or races who struggle with the same barriers to equality, by focusing attention on working-class issues, such as full employment, a living wage and social welfare programs that provide economic security, affordable housing and health care that directly affect them.

It needs to be pointed out that not all people's organizations support policies for social justice. In most communities there are taxpayer organizations dedicated to keeping taxes low and that want to reduce funding for human services and social welfare entitlements. Laissez-faire conservatives heavily support these organizations. There are other groups that oppose racial and ethnic integration, as they want to maintain social distance from groups with low social status.

There are also organizations built around the participation of clients and consumers of services. These have been most successful in organizing the consumers of health services, such as those with chronic health problems and the handicapped. Most of these health problems transcend class lines and involve families with social status and leadership experience. Also, these are generally stable populations, and their health problems and handicaps engender empathy from those who realize that it could have happened to them. Some of the most effective consumer organizations have been those serving people with intellectual and mental disabilities, cerebral palsy, and sensory handicaps such as deafness and blindness, among others. These groups have been able to improve services, especially in getting needed special education and community care. Other consumer groups in the area of education are parent-teacher organizations that have been helpful in advocating for improved schools.

In the 1960s, as a part of the poverty program, there were efforts to organize welfare recipients in what was called the welfare rights movement. The movement organized recipients for demonstrations to testify at public hearings, to lobby for legislation, and to talk to other groups concerned with the problem of poverty. One payoff was that individual recipients were provided with advocates to help them get the services they needed, and to assure them of consistent treatment rather than arbitrary actions. The main welfare rights movement was a spinoff of the civil rights movement, and its main source of support was from those who supported civil rights. Some looked at this as a form of therapy for the poor, to give them a feeling of empowerment and the hope to strive to get themselves out of poverty. The problem was that welfare recipients had difficulty finding common ground on issues of racial oppression (Nadasen, 2005). They were heavily concentrated in a few legislative districts that deprived them of a broad base of support. Often when effective leaders emerged, they were hired for jobs in human service areas. The backlash against the civil rights movement in the 1970s affected the support of welfare rights groups, and they proved powerless to prevent the punitive welfare cuts that followed. Now it would seem that the main effort should be to include welfare recipients as participants in advocacy organizations dealing with poverty concerns.

Advocacy groups have to constantly struggle for funding, which includes individual gifts and foundation grants, among other sources of revenue, through a wide variety of fundraising activities. Many advocacy groups have been able to get some funding from United Ways. Those relying heavily on grants that tend to be time-limited have often have struggled to continue. Most seek endowment funds and more longterm commitments from foundations. Public funding for advocacy is opposed by many groups, especially by conservatives who do not support their objectives and feel strongly that public taxes should not be used to advocate for public policies. There has been some public funding of neighborhood organizations, partly as a means of reducing poverty and improving neighborhood conditions, as was done in the poverty program. Individuals and groups concerned with public programs dealing with social justice need to consider contributing heavily to supporting organizations advocating for public policies, in preference to gifts to private charities that only can provide a portion of what is needed. An example is the national organization Bread for the World, which largely advocates for national legislation such as the Farm Bill, which would provide many more millions in aid for food programs than that provided by private organizations such as Oxfam.

Electoral Politics

To win elections, political parties must seek support from a variety of population groups with varied interests, and hence do not represent a single ideology. They are generally divided to the extent they seek support from those who would benefit by more liberal policies or by more conservative ones, with a lot of struggle to catch the independent vote that decides many elections. This challenges those concerned with public policy to advocate changes that are not too extreme, as was illustrated in the recent health care reform debate. In the U.S., the Democratic Party tries to appeal more to the concerns of the working class, and hence tends to be more supportive of social justice objectives; but the more conservative Republicans have supported such social welfare policies as the earned income tax credit (EITC) and the McCain proposal for a universal income tax credit for health insurance premiums. The important point is that the struggle for social justice cannot involve unwavering support for one political party and needs to consider which policies can garner more bi-partisan support.

Many private organizations seek support from donors who want to make their charitable contribution tax deductible, which requires that the contribution cannot be used for electoral purposes. This does not prevent private charities from advocating for legislative actions. Thus for action in election politics there needs to be special political action organizations. There are a number of these on the state and national level, such as MoveOn, ACORN, and the

Tea Party, and various political action committees that are most inclined to support either the Democratic or Republican party. They raise money, send out mailings, feature political ads on television and in the press, and make phone calls to urge people to register and vote for the candidates they support. In the recent national election, such organizations as MoveOn were able to make use of the Internet to raise funds and urge persons to attend meetings and rallies, to register, and to vote. These organizations have made a significant impact on the election campaigns organized by political parties and candidates.

The increased use of television, other media and mailings has greatly increased the cost of political campaigns, and there is growing recognition of how much this is influencing elections and public policy decision. A good example is the pharmaceutical industry, which has poured huge funds into election campaigns and lobbied successfully for policies they want, such as no public control of drug prices. Conservatives, as the party of the wealthy and businesses, have vast economic resources they can command for these purposes. This has certainly been a factor in their increasing political power, and has resulted in increased efforts for campaign finance reform and the establishment of state and federal election commissions to promote fairer election policies. Efforts to restrict contributions by businesses and trade unions have resulted in the creation of special political action funds, but such efforts have not done much to solve the problem. Courts have also been reluctant to curb political contributions on the basis that this interferes with the right of free speech. This view received a boost from a 2010 decision by the U.S. Supreme Court (*Citizens United v. Federal Election Commission*) that extended the right of free speech to business and union organizations that many feel was a setback for election reform. On the federal level there have been limits on contributions to election campaigns and requirements to report the extent of political contributions. More recently this has been extended to issue ads that clearly support a candidate. The federal government and some states have used the device of restricting what candidates can spend if they accept public funding. Many feel that this has been successful, mainly by making it possible for those with less financial means to run for public office and has lessened the influence of big givers. There have also been limits on financial contributions by lobbyists. It is difficult to know how much regulation will work. For example the recent action by Congress to limit contributions by lobbyists may slow this down; but lobbyists will no doubt find other ways to do the same thing. Perhaps the U.S. could follow the example of other countries by restricting the amount of television advertising in political campaigns and giving parties equal television time.

Chapter 9
Conclusion

The struggle for social justice is defined here as basically between the need of individuals and social groups for social dominance on the one hand and the need for togetherness, equality and sharing on the other. Social justice is seen as an expression of the need for togetherness that involves recognition of the dignity and worth of all individuals and gives all the right to be treated as equal in terms of civil and economic rights. In capitalist societies this largely takes the form of the struggle between different socio-economic groups, which is largely a result of the ever-increasing inequality between the owners and managers of capital and the workers they employ in the production of goods and services.

The struggle is seen as basically between the competing ideologies of laissez-faire conservatism and social liberalism. Laissez-faire conservatism is based on the concept of the unregulated free market that establishes a just price in accordance with demand and supply, and that results in the allocation of goods and services where they are most needed. The amount of wages paid are seen as rewarding the fit, those whose services are most valuable in terms of the value added by their labor. Inequality is seen as necessary in order to provide incentives to strive to render more valuable services by working harder and acquiring more needed skills. Hence, competition in the labor market results in both winners and losers, and the resulting inequality is seen as necessary to the efficient functioning of the system.

Social liberalism draws on the ideology of a democratic society that seeks both civil and economic equality, social security, and human rights, especially as stated in the Universal Declaration of Human Rights. It is concerned with economic and social conditions of various social categories, including racial and ethnic groups, men, women, children, the aged, various occupational groups, and the unemployed. It believes that more equality of income will lead to a more just society, will foster economic growth and a more equal allocation of goods and services, and that these objectives can be accomplished mainly by the use of public policies. Social liberalism relies on the concepts of macro-economic analysis, especially the circular flow of income that creates a demand for goods and services that, in turn, produces income for suppliers of these services and results in more demand. Hence, economic growth occurs when people have more money to spend. Increased productivity lowers the wage-cost per unit of the product, permitting wages to be increased without increasing prices.

Macro-economic analysis shows that employment and wages are the consequence of the functioning of the economy, and should not be blamed on the victims of unemployment or on those forced to take low-income jobs. It believes that the functioning of the economy can be shaped by public fiscal and monetary policies and that social welfare policies are not just a means of providing for economic rights, but are a means of increasing income that stimulates the economy. The functioning of the free market that sets just prices and just wages by balancing supply and demand only works with perfect competition in an economy where there are a multitude of suppliers and sources of demand, so that the action of no one can affect the price. As Galbraith (1993) pointed out, perfect market conditions may occur in settings such as the stock market and the commodity market but less so in the manufacturing system, which is often dominated by a few large corporations that do not engage in much price competition and pay wages they have established among themselves for various forms of labor. However, prices are affected by the competition for other products and services, so that suppliers have to provide cheaper products such as low-priced autos and computers that more people can afford. There is a need for public subsidies for essential items such as housing and medical care, so that low-income people can afford them, and for public aid to suppliers, mainly through tax concessions, so that they can charge less and still make a profit. Public bailout of large companies faced with bankruptcy was needed as they were seen as too big to fail without harming the economy.

Hence, comprehensive policy actions need to be considered by looking at the various systems involved. The basic systems selected here include the employment, wages and labor relations system; the social welfare system, including occupational benefits and fiscal welfare that provides both cash benefits and special in-kind benefits for the provision of food, housing and health programs; the education and infrastructure system; and the civil rights and civil liberties system. Policy actions in each system need to be considered in their proper perspective and their effects on the operation of other systems needs to be understood. A comprehensive view helps us to see where policy developments in the struggle for social justice are most needed and most feasible. Without these considerations policy actions may be counterproductive and less effective.

Particularly important is to look at the functioning of the employment, wages, and labor relations system. This calls for the use of macro-economic analysis that sees employment and economic growth as mainly the result of increases in the aggregate demands for goods and services. As the lingering 2007 economic recession has shown, the problem of unemployment is best dealt with by economic stimulus that increases aggregate demand. This calls for public policies that increase public spending, cut taxes and increase credit and investments. In dealing with public policies for the provision of health care, the health care system needs to be seen as a major factor in expanding employment, and at higher wages for those with needed skills. Hence, increased expenditures for health care results in an expanding economy rather than an economic drag. Similarly, increased social welfare expenditures result in increased spending that stimulates the economy. A good example is the U. S. Department of Agriculture's food stamp program (SNAP), which increases the sale of farm products. During economic hardship, the social welfare system is an important means of economic stability, by providing benefits that make up for lost income due to unemployment and other factors.

There are problems in regarding equality of opportunity to compete for scarce jobs as substituting for programs to increase employment. As was pointed out, this has resulted in blaming the victim for lack of attributes needed to compete, and has overemphasized education as a means of increasing employment and economic growth. The increased competition for scarce jobs led to a backlash against the advocacy of equal opportunity in the civil rights movement by those who feared they would be displaced by increased competition. Thus, job integration for racial and ethnic groups and for women is best accomplished by affirmative action based on inclusiveness, not displacement. Affirmative action works best in an expanding economy with less displacement. What macro-economic analysis also indicates is that higher wages, particularly when they are a result of greater productivity, are a vital means of increasing the demand for goods and services that results in economic growth. Thus, policies that increase wages and support the labor movement are key factors in economic growth.

A comprehensive analysis shows the importance of economic security in attaining social justice, and points to the need to expand seniority protection for workers and to provide for public and private insurance systems that protect against loss of income due to such things as retirement, unemployment, illness and disability. One of the basic functions of the social welfare system is to provide all people entitlement to basic human rights, through social insurance and other fiscal, occupational and social welfare benefits that provide a decent standard of living for the working, the unemployed, the retired, the sick, the disabled, and their dependents. It is important to recognize that the emphasis must be on entitlements to basic human rights, rather than on just safety-net protection for the poor that the conservatives advocate. With the Temporary Assistance for Needy Families (TANF) program limited by Clinton-era "reforms," many struggling with unemployment and living in poverty are only entitled to the safety net of food stamps and emergency medical care (Pavetti & Rosenbaum, 2010).

This shredded safety net has been mainly applied to services that help the working poor under the guise that a large pool of low-paid workers are without the opportunity to pursue higher education. Many TANF recipients are limited to low-income and part-time jobs that still do not provide an adequate income (Alfred, 2007; Lower-Basch, 2011). As many who have examined welfare cuts have noted, they have clear racial overtones that oppress racial minorities (Reisch & Sommerfeld, 2002; Savner, 2000). There has been a failure to provide for basic human rights called for in the Universal Declaration of Human Rights for such things as jobs and an income that provides a decent standard of living, including the provision of nutrition, housing and medical care. The deprivation of human rights through cuts in welfare benefits must be condemned as a form of human oppression. In this connection, there needs to be awareness of the concept of mystification that occurs when the agents of the oppressors provide token aid to the oppressed, so that they appear to be loving, caring persons. It would seem that most soup kitchens, token handouts and gifts to the poor at Christmas are examples of mystification.

The provision of social welfare benefits raises the issue that taxes are needed to finance them. Social insurance such as Social Security can be best handled through a payroll tax paid by the employer and the employee and placed into a special trust fund out of which benefits are paid. Funding other social welfare benefits for such things as income subsidies, affordable housing and medical care, which serve to redistribute income, can best be accomplished by a progressive income tax. One way to pay benefits is by the use of an income tax credit with a refund to those who do not owe enough in taxes to receive the full benefit. An income tax credit is an effective way of combining taxes and benefits; it can be done through one piece of tax legislation that combines the credit with the needed increase in income tax rates in order to make up for lost revenue. EITC programs are used to subsidize wages mostly for those with dependent children, and have had bi-partisan support at the federal and state levels. Income tax credits have been advocated as a means of subsidizing medical insurance costs for all in order to provide universal health care. The income tax credit draws on the concept of a negative income tax that uses a refund as a means of providing for those who lack the income needed for a basic standard of living.

Conservatives want to maintain the private economy as the prime means of providing goods and services, and hence want public funds for social welfare services provided to for-profit and nonprofit agencies through grants, service contracts and purchase of service agreements. This is extensively done in the public funding of hospitals, nursing homes and other forms of medical care, housing projects, and childcare. This raises many complicated issues as to the rates paid, the quality of services rendered, salaries paid, and accountability in the use of public funds by private agencies.

Extremely vital in the struggle for social justice and equality is education. However, the push for attaining higher education will not lead to equality if jobs cannot be found in a struggling economy. There has been a focus on the academic achievement gap as it relates to socioeconomic status, and a focus on improving the educational system as a crucial factor in achieving social justice that needs to be examined. As has been extensively discussed, education attainment is seen as a means of providing equality of opportunity to compete for scarce jobs; it does not do much, however, to increase overall employment, to eliminate low-income jobs or to prevent the outsourcing of high-wage jobs to other countries. Raising the general level of education tends to lead to more productivity and, hence, to higher wages; but an increase in the supply of well-educated people makes it possible to fill positions with such people with only a small increase in pay. The level of educational attainment needed for higher wages and the skills and knowledge required for good paying, skilled jobs results in more stratification not greater equality. Hence, more equality of income is best achieved by corrective actions in the functioning of the labor market, including collective bargaining by trade unions, public policies that set minimum wages, wages paid in government contracts, and social welfare programs that transfer income.

Education, particularly postsecondary professional and technical education, is a vital factor in increasing productivity that leads to economic growth and a higher standard of living. It is important to remember that educational attainment is affected by economic inequality, and that poverty and low-incomes create instability and hopelessness, which hampers the educational process and hurts equality of opportunity. Thus, what is needed is to stop blaming schools and teachers for the lack of educational progress of low-income children and instead provide for economic security and a decent standard of living for all. Also it is important to remember that socio-economic integration of schools improves school performance and, hence, there needs to be further efforts to accomplish integration by the use of magnet and other special schools (Schwartz, 2010). Primarily at the tertiary level, affirmative action is needed so that racial minorities are admitted and enrolled in programs where they are vastly underrepresented.

Civil rights and civil liberties are an important element in the struggle for social justice. As was noted, major achievements in this struggle were the abolition of slavery, voting rights for women and the federal Civil Rights Act and the Voting Rights Act. The federal Civil Rights Act and subsequent state and local laws sought to eliminate discrimination in employment and in most aspects of public and private life. The main problem is that women and racial and ethnic minorities have largely been relegated to relatively low-income jobs, especially in the service sector. This has given rise to the use of affirmative action programs to include more women and minorities in jobs filled predominately by white males. This has been more successful for women than for racial minorities. The income gap has been closing between men and women, as women have moved into many professional jobs that were traditionally male, including medicine, law, and business. Women have the strength of numbers and have been less hurt by the decline in manufacturing and less disadvantaged by low class status that affects the level of education and sophistication sought in many employments.

Racial differences, especially for African Americans, feed the social dominance needs of most whites who seek to maintain various forms of social and economic distance. Much of this dominance has roots in slavery, which deprived African Americans of basic human rights. Hence, racism has been a major factor to overcome in the struggle for social justice. The main problem is the failure to close the income gap between African Americans and whites, despite increased educational attainment for African Americans. Also, as of the middle of 2012, the unemployment rate for African Americans remains almost double that of whites, at 13.6 percent compared to 7.4 percent (Luhby, 2012). African Americans are still largely relegated to low-income service jobs and have been especially hurt by the decline in manufacturing jobs. This situation represents a real challenge to develop effective affirmative action programs in education and employment. Progress will not be rapid due to the opposition of those whites who feel that this will threaten their status. Much of this opposition can be alleviated if all are assured of greater economic security.

All of these efforts to analyze and evaluate needed policies must lead to actions to implement them. This largely requires actions that affect the political decision-making process, by mustering a strong base of support. As was emphasized, this calls for developing universal policies, such as the social insurances, tax credits, economic growth, full employment and policies for human rights—both civil and economic—rather than on selective policies that focus on poverty and the poor. Policies that single out the poor are affected by how people identify with the poor and can lead to policies that blame the victim and result in token and punitive actions (Daly, 1996). Building a broad base of support for universal policies largely requires organizing various population groups that will benefit by them. This calls for mobilizing various occupational groups such as trade unions and other employee organizations. Other groups that it has been possible to organize are the aged, women, and various minorities. Organizing the consumers of services has been effective when they cut across class lines, as is the case with the handicapped. Political campaigns have been successful, as was illustrated by the 2008 Obama campaign, when they employ a populist strategy that appeals to the middle class in addition to the working class.

Summary

It needs to be recognized that the quest for social justice is always a struggle against powerful forces that want to maintain their social dominance. It is especially a hard struggle in a country such as the United States with its racial and ethnic heterogeneous population that works against a spirit of togetherness. This country's large size makes for regional differences between the Rust Belt and the South that further contributes to the struggle. Recently, the struggle has become more difficult due to the rapid pace of changes in the economy and the labor market, including globalization and the loss of manufacturing jobs. As a result, the weakened labor movement has become a lesser force in the struggle, inequalities have increased and economic security is under attack.

The challenge is immense. This book emphasized changing policy goals—from reducing poverty to entitlement to basic human rights—both civil and economic. The focus on poverty has degenerated into blaming the poor and shredding the safety net that has resulted in oppressive cuts in welfare benefits. The conservatives are using their increasing power to oppose the establishment of human rights that are costly and affect their social dominance. In addition to ending federal public assistance programs to families with children as an entitlement, they want to continue on this path starting with the federal entitlement to Medicare and Medicaid, eventually ending all federal entitlements.

Welfare reforms should be countered by putting the chronic unemployed to work in a way that will restore the entitlement. What is further advocated here is the use of the Declaration of Human Rights as a basis for policy actions for entitlements, especially federal entitlements. Real social justice rests on national policy actions. The challenge is immense and will require developing strong coalitions that will deal with the struggle comprehensively, with a clear sense of priorities as to what is needed and politically feasible.

For now the main effort may be in defending what currently exists. It is well to end here with the statement in section 25 of the Universal Declaration of Human Rights that has been used here several times. It states:

"Everyone has the right to a standard of living adequate for the health and well-being of himself and of his family, including food, clothing, housing and medical care and necessary social services, and the right to security in the event of unemployment, sickness, disability, widowhood, old age or other lack of livelihood in circumstances beyond his control."

What is needed is the conviction that this is an expression of God-given truths as to universal human needs and rights and that, in the words of Battle Hymn of the Republic, "His truth is marching on."

219

References

AARP. (2004). *Retirement income*. (The Policy Book: AARP Public Policies). Retrieved from http://assets.aarp.org/www.aarp.org/ articles/legpolicy/3_retinc.pdf.

Abramovitz, M. (1986). The privatization of the welfare state: A review. *Social Work, 31*(4), 257-264.

Akamatsu, K. (1962, March-August). A historical pattern of economic growth in developing countries. *Journal of Developing Economies, 1*(1), 3-25.

Alfred, M.V. (2007, August). Welfare reform and black women's economic development. *Adult Education Quarterly, 57*(4), 293-311.

Anderson, A. (2010, July). *No free lunch: Tax cuts widen budget gaps* (Budget Brief). Sacramento, CA: California Budget Project. Retrieved from http://cbp.org/pdfs/2010/100707_No_- Free_Lunch_bb.pdf.

Annie E. Casey Foundation. (2006a). Unequal opportunity within criminal justice (fact sheet). *Race Matters: What's Race Got To Do With It?* Retrieved from http://www.aecf.org/upload/pub- licationfiles/fact_sheet13.pdf.

Annie E. Casey Foundation. (2006b). Unequal opportunities for income security (fact sheet). *Race Matters: What's Race Got To Do With It?* Retrieved from http://www.aecf.org/upload/- publicationfiles/fact_sheet6.pdf.

Appleby, J. (2007, November 12). Employer-provided insur- ance continues to decline. *USA Today*. Retrieved from http://www.usatoday.com/money/industries/insurance/2007-11-12- social-net_N.htm.

Arnold, D.G., & Bowie, N.E. (2003, April). Sweatshops and respect for persons. *Business Ethics Quarterly, 13*(2), 221-242.

Australian Government. (2008). *The guide: CSA's online guide to the administration of the new child support scheme*. Retrieved from http://guide.csa.gov.au/.

Baumol, W.J. & Blinder, A.S. (2009). *Economics, principles and policy* (11th ed.). Mason, OH: South-Western Cengage Learning.

Bloom, D., Scrivener, S., Michalopoulos, C., Morris, P., Hendra, R., Adams-Ciardullo, D., Walter, J., & Vargas, W. (2002, February). *Jobs first: Final report on Connecticut's welfare reform initiative*. New York, NY: Manpower Demonstration Research Corporation. Retrieved from http://www.mdrc.org/publications-/90/full.pdf.

Board of Trustees of the Federal Old-Age and Survivors Insurance and Federal Disability Trust Funds. (2011). *Annual report of the Board of Trustees of the Federal Old-Age and Survivors Insurance Federal Disability Trust Funds*. H.R. Doc. (112-23). Retrieved from http://www.ssa.gov/OACT/TR/2011/tr2011.pdf.

Brinkley, A. (2010, June 21). Henry Luce: The master of a changing media landscape. *History News Network*. Retrieved from http://hnn.us/articles/128108.html.

Brown, J.P. (2010, June 19). Election of first female head endorsed by Episcopal rector. *Kentucky New Era*. Retrieved from http://www.kentuckynewera.com/web/news/article_346b8405-7456-5f07-b40b-5da16c6a1a67.html.

Buss, T.F. (2001). The effect of state tax incentives on economic growth and firm location decisions: An overview of the literature. *Economic Development Quarterly, 15*(1), 90-105.

Cancian, M. (2001). Rhetoric and reality of work-based welfare reform. *Social Work, 46*(4), 309.

Card, D. & Krueger, A.B. (1994, September). Minimum wages and employment: A case study of the fast-food industry in New Jersey and Pennsylvania. *American Economic Review, 84*(4), 772-93.

Cascio, W.F. (2002). *Responsible restructuring: Creative and profitable alternatives to layoffs*. San Francisco, CA: Berrett-Koehler Publishers, Inc.

Cauthen, N.K. (2006). *Looking forward, looking back: Reflections on the 10th anniversary of welfare reform*. New York, NY: National Center for Children in Poverty, School of Public Health.

Cattaneo, M.D., Galiani, S., Gertler, P.J., Martinez, S., & Titiunik, R. (2009, February). Housing, health, and happiness. *American Economic Journal: Economic Policy, 1*(1), 75-105.

Christie, Les. (2010, July 30). *Pay gap persists for African-Americans*. CNN Money. Retrieved from http://money.cnn.com/-2010/07/30/news/economy/black_pay_gap_persists/index.htm.

Cohen, A. (1969, June). Political anthropology: The analysis of the symbolism of power relations. *Man*, New Series, *4*(2), 215-235.

Cohn, D. & Livingston, G. (2010, April 6). *U.S. birth rate decline linked to recession*. Washington, D.C.: Pew Research Center. Retrieved from http://pewsocialtrends.org/2010/04/06/us-birth-rate-decline-linked-to-recession/.

Collins, C. & Yeskel, F. (2005). *Economic apartheid in America*. New York, NY: The New Press.

Congressional Budget Office. (2004, August). *Effective federal tax rates under current law, 2001 to 2014*. Washington, D.C. Retrieved from http://www.cbo.gov/ftpdocs/57xx/doc5746/08-13-EffectiveFedTaxRates.pdf.

Connecticut Judicial Branch. (1999). *Milo Sheff, et al.: Complex litigation docket v.: at New Britain William A. O'Neill: Memorandum of Decision*. Retrieved from http://www.jud.ct.gov/external/news/sheff.htm.

Daly, G. (1996). *Homeless: Policies, strategies, and lives on the street*. New York, NY: Routledge.

DeNavas-Walt, C., Proctor, B.D., & Smith, J.C. (2010, September). U.S. Census Bureau, Current Population Reports: Consumer Income, 60-238. *Income, poverty, and health insurance coverage in the United States: 2009.* Washington, D.C. U.S. Government Printing Office. Retrieved from http://www.census.gov/-prod/2010pubs/p60-238.pdf.

DeWitt, L. (2005, March 4). *The social security trust funds and the federal budget.* Baltimore, MD: Social Security Act Historian's Office. Retrieved from http://www.ssa.gov/history/Budget-Treatment.html.

Dorus, M.B. & Roberts, D.F. (2002). Welfare reform and families in the child welfare system. *Maryland Law Review, 61*(2).

Engel, M. (2010, June 4). The real unemployment rate? 16.6%. *MSN Money.* Retrieved from http://articles.moneycentral.-msn.com/learn-how-to-invest/The-real-unemployment-rate.aspx.

Fisher, E.S. (2007, May 3). Too old to hire, too young to retire. *Westchester Magazine.* Retrieved from http://www.west-chestermagazine.com/Westchester-Magazine/June-2006/Too-Old-to-Hire-Too-Young-to-Retire/.

Galbraith, J.K. (1993). *American capitalism: The concept of countervailing power.* New Brunswick, NJ: Transaction Publishers.

Galbraith, J.K. (1996). *The good society: The humane agenda.* Boston, MA: Houghton Mifflin Company.

Gittell, R. & Rudokas, J. (2007). *New England has the highest increase in income disparity in the nation.* Carsey Institute: New England Issue Brief (4). Retrieved from http://www.carsey-institute.unh.edu/publications/IB_incomeinequality_07.pdf.

Gross, A. & Tran, C. (2003, Oct.). Economic challenges spur nontraditional employment in Japan. *Society for Human Resources Management Global Perspectives.* Pacific Bridge. Retrieved from http://www.pacificbridge.com/publication.asp?id=27.

Hirsch, B.T., Macpherson, D.A., & Vroman, W.G. (2001, July). Estimates of union density by state. *Monthly Labor Review, 124*(7), 51-55.

Hagenbaugh, B. (2009, April 9). Many of the jobless get no unemployment benefits. *USA Today.* Retrieved from http://www.-

usatoday.com/money/economy/employment/20090409unemploy-ed-but-no-benefits_N.htm.

Harrington, P.E. & Sum, A.M. (2010, November 8). College labor shortages in 2018? *The New England Journal of Higher Education.* Boston, MA: New England Board of Higher Education. Retrieved from http://www.nebhe.org/2010/11/08/college-labor-shortages-in-2018/.

Herbert, B. (2003, June 2). The reverse Robin Hood. *The New York Times.* Retrieved from http://www.nytimes.com/2003/06/02/-opinion/the-reverse-robin-hood.html.

Hernandez-Murillo, R. & Roisman, D. (n.d.). *The economics of charitable giving: What gives?.* Retrieved from http://faculty.-pepperdine.edu/jburke2/giving.pdf.

Hero, J. (2007, October). *Connecticut leads the nation in multiple measures of income inequality.* New Haven, CT: Connecticut Voices for Children. Retrieved from http://www.ctdatahaven.org-/reports/CT_inequality_07.pdf.

Human Resources and Skills Development Canada. (1994, November). *Wage subsidies to encourage the hiring of unemployment insurance claimants.* Retrieved from http://www.-hrsdc.gc.ca/eng/cs/sp/hrsd/prc/publications/research/1998-00026-/page06.shtml.

Institute on Taxation and Economic Policy. (2009, November). *Who pays? A distribution analysis of the tax system in all 50 states.* Retrieved from http://www.itepnet.org/whopays3.pdf.

Internal Revenue Service. (2011). *Tax year 2010 and preview tax year 2011.* Retrieved from http://www.eitc.irs.gov/central/Preview2009/.

Irving, F. (2009, August). Serving rural patients. *ADVANCE for Health Information Executives*, 13(8), 18-22. Retrieved from http://www.carefx.com/xres/uploads/news-documents/LARHIX_-Cover_Story.pdf.

Johnson, P.A. (2011). *Charity and justice* (PA Anti-Poverty Summit). Harrisburg, PA: UMC Advocacy. Retrieved from http://www.umadvocacypa.org/node/37.

Johnson, D.C. & Salle, L.M. (2004, November). *Responding to the attack on public education and teacher unions.* Menlo Park, CA: The Commonweal Institute. Retrieved from http://www.commonwealinstitute.org/cw/files/Responding_Ed_Report%20fro m%20CI%20website_0.pdf.

Kahlenberg, R.D. (2003). *All together now: Creating middle-class schools through public school choice.* Washington, D.C.: Brookings Institute Press.

Keynes, J.M. (2006). *The general theory of employment, interest, and money.* Rajouri Garden, New Dalhi: Atlantic Publishers and Distributors.

Kingson, E.R. (1996). Ways of thinking about the long-term care of the baby-boom cohorts. *Journal of Aging & Social Policy,* *7*(3/4), 3-23.

Kuttner, R. (1992). *The end of laissez faire: National purpose and the global economy after the cold war.* Philadelphia, PA: University of Pennsylvania Press.

Kuttner, R. (1999). *Everything for sale: The virtues and limits of markets.* Chicago, IL: The University of Chicago Press.

Lower-Basch, E. (2011, January 24). *TANF policy brief: Goals for TANF reauthorization.* Washington, DC: Center for Law and Social Policy (CLASP). Retrieved from http://www.clasp.org/-admin/site/publications/files/TANF-Reauthorization-Goals.pdf.

Luhby, T. (2012, June 21). *Worsening wealth inequality by race.* CNN Money. Retrieved from http://money.cnn.com/2012/06-/21/news/economy/wealth-gap-race/index.htm.

MacArthur Foundation, John D. and Catherine T. (2005, Spring). Revitalizing bronzeville: Mixed-income housing is key to community strength. *Housing Matters,* 1, 8-11. Retrieved from http://www.macfound.org/atf/cf/%7BB0386CE3-8B29-4162-8098-E466FB856794%7D/spring05.pdf.

Massey, D. (2007). *Categorically unequal: The American stratification system*. New York, NY: Russell Sage Foundation.

McFadden, D.L. (n.d.). *The economics of social security reform* (Working Paper). Retrieved from http://elsa.berkeley.-edu/wp/mcfadden0105/SocialSecurityMcFadden.pdf.

Nadasen, P. (2005). *Welfare warriors: The welfare rights movement in the United States*. New York, NY: Routledge.

National Coalition for the Homeless. (2007, August). *Homeless families with children: NCH fact sheet #12*. Retrieved from http://www.nationalhomeless.org/publications/facts/families.html.

National Conference of State Legislatures. (2008, February). *Highlights of recent kinship care state legislative enactments*. Retrieved from http://www.ncsl.org/IssuesResearch/Human-Services/HIGHLIGHTSOFRECENTKINSHIPCARESTATELEGI SLATIV/tabid/16371/Default.aspx.

National Low Income Housing Coalition. (2010). *Out of reach 2010: Connecticut*. Retrieved from http://www.nlihc.org/oor/oor-2010/data.cfm?getstate=on&state=CT.

Neubeck, K.J. & Cazenave, N.A. (2001). *Welfare racism: Playing the race card against America's poor*. New York, NY: Routledge.

New, M.J. (2009, Fall). Starve the beast: A further examination. *Cato Journal, 29*(3), 487-495.

Olson, D.J. & Steinman, E. (2004). Evaluating the living-wage strategy: Prospects, problems, and possibilities. In Simmons, L. (Ed.), *Welfare, the working poor, and labor*. Armonk, New York: M.E. Sharpe, Inc.

Partnership for Strong Communities. (2011, February 23). *Obama budget: HUD programs fall below FY11 requested levels*. Retrieved from http://www.ctpartnershiphousing.com/index.php?-option=com_content&task=view&id=1898&Itemid=40.

Partnership for Strong Communities. (2010, July 6). *State's 8-30g affordable housing appeals procedure turns 20*. Retrieved from http://www.ctpartnershiphousing.com/index.php?option=-com_content&task=view&id=1551&Itemid=119.

Parrot, S., & Sherman, A. (2006). *TANF at 10, program results are more mixed than often understood.* Washington, D.C.: Center on Budget and Policy Priorities.

Pavetti, L., & Rosenbaum, D. (2010, February 25). *Creating a safety net that works when the economy doesn't: The role of the food stamp and TANF programs.* Washington, D.C.: Center on Budget and Policy Priorities. Retrieved from http://www.cbpp.org/cms/index.cfm?fa=view&id=3096.

PBS Home Video. (1999). Crucible of empire: The Spanish-American war [*Television broadcast*].

Pearce, D. & Brooks, J. (2002, September). *The self-sufficiency standard for Florida.* Retrieved from http://www.wow-online.org/ourprograms/fess/state-resources/SSS/The%20Self-Sufficiency%20Standard%20for%20Florida.pdf

Pew Research Center. (2008, February). *U.S. religious landscape survey religious affiliation: Diverse and dynamic.* Washington, D.C.: Pew Forum on Religion & Public Life. Retrieved from http://religions.pewforum.org/pdf/report-religious-landscape-study-full.pdf.

Phillips, K. (1990). *The politics of rich and poor: Wealth and the American electorate in the Reagan aftermath.* New York, NY: Basic Books.

Pitts, L. (2006). *Becoming dad: Black men and the journey to fatherhood.* Evanston, IL: Agate Publishing, Inc.

Piven, F.P. & Cloward, R. (1993). *Regulating the poor: The functions of public welfare* (2nd ed.). New York, NY: Vintage Books.

Progressive States Network. (n.d.). *State policy options for promoting affordable housing.* Retrieved from http://smartgrowthamerica.org/RP_docs/PSN_housing_statepolicy.pdf.

Rahm, D. & Coggburn, J.D. (2007, October). Environmentally preferable procurement: Greening U.S. state government fleets. *Public Works Management Policy, 12*(2), 400-415.

Ravitch, D. (2010). *The death and life of the great American school system: How testing and choice are undermining education.* New York, NY: Basic Books.

Reisch, M. & Sommerfeld, D. (2002). Race, welfare reform and nonprofit organizations. *Journal of Sociology and Social Welfare, 24*(1), 155-177.

Results. (2011). *Child tax credit.* Washington, D.C. Retrieved from http://www.results.org/issues/us_poverty_campaigns/economic_ opportuntyfor_all/child_tax_credit/

Rice, D. & Sard, B. (2007, February 1). *Cuts in federal housing assistance are undermining community plans to end homelessness.* Washington, D.C.: Center on Budget and Policy Priorities. Retrieved from http://www.cbpp.org/cms/index.cfm?fa=view&id=1038

Rietmulder, M. (2011, January 25). *GOP's reverse-Robin Hood approach: Asking Minnesotans to pay more in tuition and taxes while cutting the corporate income tax is misguided.* Minnesota Daily. Retrieved from http://www.mndaily.com/2011/01/25/-gops-reverse-robin-hood-approach.

Rodrik, D. (2000, December). Growth versus poverty reduction: A hollow debate. *Finance and Development, 37*(4).

Rosenblatt, R.A. & Hart, L.G. (2000, November). Physicians and rural America. *The Western Journal of Medicine, 173*(5), 348-351.

Rotherham, A.J. (2010, October 28). School of thought: Does income-based school integration work? *Time.* Retrieved from http://www.time.com/time/nation/article/0,8599,2027858,00.html.

Ryan, W. (1971). *Blaming the victim.* New York, NY: Pantheon Books.

Sabin, J. (1997). Organized psychiatry and managed care, quality improvement or holy war? *Health Affairs, 161*, 22-33.

Savner, S. (2000, July-August). Welfare reform and racial/ethnic minorities: The questions to ask. *Race & Poverty, 9*, 3-5.

Sawicky, M.B. (2004). The mirage of welfare reform. In Simmons, L. (Ed.), *Welfare, the working poor, and labor*. Armonk, NY: M.E. Sharpe, Inc.

Schmitt, J. & Zipperer, B. (2008, February). *The decline in African-American representation in unions and manufacturing, 1979-2007* (Issue Brief). Washington, D.C.: Center for Economic and Policy Research. Retrieved from http://www.cepr.net/documents/publications/unions_aa_2008_02.pdf.

Scherr, A. (1966). *Poor kids*. New York, NY: Basic Books.

Schwartz, H. (2010). *Housing policy is school policy: Economically integrative housing promotes academic success in Montgomery County, Maryland*. New York, NY: Century Foundation. Retrieved from http://tcf.org/publications/pdfs/housing-policy-is-school-policy-pdf/Schwartz.pdf

Shapiro, I. (1992). *Far from fixed: An analysis of the unemployment insurance system*. Center on Budget and Policy Priorities.

Shaw, G.B. (1951). *Pygmalion*. Baltimore, MD: Penguin Books.

Shonkoff, J.P. & Phillips, D.A. (2000). *From neurons to neighborhoods: The science of early childhood development*. Washington, D.C.: National Academy Press.

Sidanius, J. & Pratto, F. (1999). *Social Dominance: An intergroup theory of social hierarchy and oppression*. Cambridge, UK: Cambridge University Press.

Smith, L. (2011, March 22). Rural health: If you build it, will specialists come? *Georgia Health News*. Retrieved from http://www.georgiahealthnews.com/2011/03/22/rural-health-build-it-specialists-come/.

Social Security Administration. (2010, October). *2011 Social Security changes*. Retrieved from http://www.ssa.gov/pressoffice/colafacts.htm.

Social Security Online. (2010, October 29). *National average wage index*. Retrieved from http://www.ssa.gov/OACT/cola/AWI.-html.

Solis, H.L. & Hall, K. (2010, December). *Women in the labor force: A databook* (report 1026). Retrieved from http://www.bls.-gov/cps/wlf-databook-2010.pdf.

Spencer, M.L., Reno, R., Powell, J.A., & Grant-Thomas, A. (2009, February). *The benefits of racial and economic integration in our education system: Why this matters for our democracy*. Columbus, OH: Kirwan Institute for the Study of Race and Ethnicity. Retrieved from http://4909e99d35cada63e7f75747-1b7243be73e53e14.gripelements.com/publications/education_integration_memo_feb2009.pdf.

Stewart, F. (2000, March). *Income distribution and development*. QEH Working Paper Series 37, Oxford University. Retrieved from http://www3.qeh.ox.ac.uk/pdf/qehwp/qehwps37.pdf.

Stowe, H.B. (1852). *Uncle tom's cabin*. Cleveland, OH: John P. Jewett Company.

Stuart, A. & Bok, M. (2003). *Welfare reform and the role of work for low-income women*. Rocky Hill, CT: National Association of Social Workers Connecticut.

Sullivan, A. (2009, September 24). Recession fallout: Fewer women having kids. *Time*. Retrieved from http://www.time.com/-time/health/article/0,8599,1925944,00.html.

Takahashi, Y. (1990). Human resource management in Japan. In R. Pieper (Ed.), *Human resource management: An international comparison* (211-232). Berlin, Germany: Walter de Gruyter & Co.

Tatum, B.D. (1997). *'Why are all the black kids sitting together in the cafeteria?': And other conversations about race*. New York, NY: Basic Books.

Tax Policy Center. (2011, April 4). *Historic effective federal tax rates for all households*. Retrieved from http://www.taxpolicy-center.org/taxfacts/displayafact.cfm?Docid=456.

Thernstrom, S. & Thernstrom, A. (1997). *America in black and white: One nation, indivisible.* New York, NY: Touchstone.

Titmuss, R.M. (1958). *Essays on 'the welfare state'.* London: George Allen & Unwin.

Towers Perrin. (2008). *2008 health care cost survey.* Retrieved from http://www.towersperrin.com/tp/getwebcachedoc?-webc=HRS/USA/2008/200801/hccs_2008.pdf.

Tracy, J. (2008, Spring). Hope VI mixed-income housing projects displace poor people. *Race, Poverty & the Environment: Who Owns Our Cities?, 15*(1), 26-29.

Trattner, W.I. (1999). *From poor law to welfare state: A history of social welfare in America* (6th ed.). New York, NY: The Free Press.

United Nations. (1948, December 10). *The universal declaration of human rights.* Retrieved from http://www.un.org/-en/documents/udhr/.

United States Department of Treasury, Internal Revenue Service. (2011). *EITC income limits, maximum credit amounts and tax law updates.* Retrieved from http://www.irs.gov/individuals/article/0,,id=150513,00.html.

United States Bureau of Labor Statistics. (2011a). *Household data annual averages.* Employed persons by occupation, race, Hispanic or Latino ethnicity, and sex. Retrieved from http://www.bls.gov/web/empsit/cpseea20.pdf.

United States Bureau of Labor Statistics. (2011b, Feb. 17). *Economy at a glance.* Retrieved from http://www.bls.gov/-eag/eag.us.htm.

United States Bureau of Labor Statistics. (2011c). *The employment situation.* Retrieved from http://www.bls.gov/news.release/pdf/empsit.pdf.

United States Bureau of Labor Statistics. (2011d, January 21). *Union membership-2010.* (News Release). Retrieved from http://www.bls.gov/news.release/pdf/union2.pdf.

United States Census Bureau. (2005, February 22). Historical Income Tables- Families. *Housing and household economic status division.* Retrieved from http://www.census.gov/hhes/www/income/histinc/f05ar.htm.

United States Census Bureau. (2011). Income, expenditures, poverty, & wealth. *The 2011 statistical abstract: The national data book.* Retrieved from http://www.census.gov/compendia/statab/-cats/income_expenditures_poverty_wealth.html.

United States Department of Agriculture. (2010, September. 10). *Supplemental nutrition assistance program: FY 2011 allotments and deduction information.* Retrieved from http://www.fns.-usda.gov/snap/government/FY11_Allot_Deduct.htm

United States Department of Housing and Urban Development. (n.d.). *Choice neighborhoods.* Retrieved from http://portal.hud.gov/hudportal/HUD?src=/program_offices/public-_indian_housing/programs/ph/cn

United States Department of Housing and Urban Development. (2010). *HUD strategic plan: FY 2010-2015.* Retrieved from http://portal.hud.gov/hudportal/documents/huddoc?id=DOC_4436-.pdf.

United States Department of Labor. (2010). *Wage and hour division.* Retrieved from http://www.dol.gov/whd/state/stateMin-WageHis.htm.

United States Department of Labor. (n.d.). *Data retrieval: Employment, hours, and earnings (CES).* Bureau of Labor Statistics. Retrieved from http://www.bls.gov/webapps/legacy/cesbtab-1.htm.

Urban Institute, The. (2006). *A decade of welfare reform: Facts and figures.* Washington, D.C.

Urrieta, L. (2004, September). Assistencialism and the politics of high-stakes testing. *The Urban Review, 36*(3), 211-226.

Vergari, S. (2007, January). The politics of charter schools. *Educational Policy, 21*(1), 15-39.

Wallis, J. (2005). *God's politics: Why the right gets it wrong and the left doesn't get it.* New York, NY: HarperCollins Publishers, Inc.

Walsh, D.J. (2010). *Employment law for human resource practice* (3rd ed.). Mason, OH: South-Western, Cengage Learning.

Wayne, L. (2002, September 1). A guardian of jobs or a 'reverse Robin Hood'? The *New York Times*. Retrieved from http://query.nytimes.com/gst/fullpage.html?res=9C02E0DA123FF932A3575AC0A9649C8B63&pagewanted=all.

Weller, C.E., Scott, R.E., & Hersh, A.S. (2003). The unremarkable record of liberalized trade. In W. Driscoll & J. Clark (Eds.), *Globalization and the poor: Exploitation or equalizer?* (32-45). New York, NY: International Debate Education Association.

Western, B. & Wildeman, C. (2009, January). The black family and mass incarceration. *The ANNALS of the American Academy of Political and Social Science, 621*(1), 221-242.

White House, The (2010a). *Ensuring that student loans are affordable.* (Fact Sheet). Retrieved from http://www.whitehouse.gov/sites/default/files/100326-ibr-fact-sheet.pdf.

White House, The. (2010b, November 17). *Executive order: Fundamental principles and policymaking criteria for partnerships with faith-based and other neighborhood organizations.* Retrieved from http://www.whitehouse.gov/the-press-office/2010/11/17/executive-order-fundamental-principles-and-policymaking-criteria-partner

Wolff, E.N., (2002). *Top heavy: inequality in America and what can be done about it* (2nd ed.). New York, NY: New Press.

Wronka, J. (1991). *Human rights and social policy in the 21st century.* Lantoon, NY: University Press of America.

Appendix:
U. N. Universal Declaration of Human Rights

(Adopted by the General Assembly of the United Nations on December 10, 1948)

PREAMBLE

Whereas recognition of the inherent dignity and of the equal and inalienable rights of all members of the human family is the foundation of freedom, justice and peace in the world,

Whereas disregard and contempt for human rights have resulted in barbarous acts which have outraged the conscience of mankind, and the advent of a world in which human beings shall enjoy freedom of speech and belief and freedom from fear and want has been proclaimed as the highest aspiration of the common people,

Whereas it is essential, if man is not to be compelled to have recourse, as a last resort, to rebellion against tyranny and oppression, that human rights should be protected by the rule of law,

Whereas it is essential to promote the development of friendly relations between nations,

Whereas the peoples of the United Nations have in the Charter reaffirmed their faith in fundamental human rights, in the dignity and worth of the human person and in the equal rights of men and women and have determined to promote social progress and better standards of life in larger freedom,

Whereas Member States have pledged themselves to achieve, in co-operation with the United Nations, the promotion of universal respect for and observance of human rights and fundamental freedoms,

Whereas a common understanding of these rights and freedoms is of the greatest importance for the full realization of this pledge,

234

Now, Therefore **THE GENERAL ASSEMBLY** proclaims **THIS UNIVERSAL DECLARATION OF HUMAN RIGHTS** as a common standard of achievement for all peoples and all nations, to the end that every individual and every organ of society, keeping this Declaration constantly in mind, shall strive by teaching and education to promote respect for these rights and freedoms and by progressive measures, national and international, to secure their universal and effective recognition and observance, both among the peoples of Member States themselves and among the peoples of territories under their jurisdiction.

Article 1

All human beings are born free and equal in dignity and rights. They are endowed with reason and conscience and should act towards one another in a spirit of brotherhood.

Article 2

Everyone is entitled to all the rights and freedoms set forth in this Declaration, without distinction of any kind, such as race, color, sex, language, religion, political or other opinion, national or social origin, property, birth or other status. Furthermore, no distinction shall be made on the basis of the political, jurisdictional or international status of the country or territory to which a person belongs, whether it be independent, trust, non-self-governing or under any other limitation of sovereignty.

Article 3

Everyone has the right to life, liberty and security of person.

Article 4

No one shall be held in slavery or servitude; slavery and the slave trade shall be prohibited in all their forms.

Article 5

No one shall be subjected to torture or to cruel, inhuman or degrading treatment or punishment.

Article 6

Everyone has the right to recognition everywhere as a person before the law.

Article 7

All are equal before the law and are entitled without any discrimination to equal protection of the law. All are entitled to equal protection against any discrimination in violation of this Declaration and against any incitement to such discrimination.

Article 8

Everyone has the right to an effective remedy by the competent national tribunals for acts violating the fundamental rights granted him by the constitution or by law.

Article 9

No one shall be subjected to arbitrary arrest, detention or exile.

Article 10

Everyone is entitled in full equality to a fair and public hearing by an independent and impartial tribunal, in the determination of his rights and obligations and of any criminal charge against him.

Article 11

(1) Everyone charged with a penal offence has the right to be presumed innocent until proved guilty according to law in a public trial at which he has had all the guarantees necessary for his defence.

(2) No one shall be held guilty of any penal offence on account of any act or omission which did not constitute a penal offence, under

national or international law, at the time when it was committed. Nor shall a heavier penalty be imposed than the one that was applicable at the time the penal offence was committed.

Article 12

No one shall be subjected to arbitrary interference with his privacy, family, home or correspondence, nor to attacks upon his honour and reputation. Everyone has the right to the protection of the law against such interference or attacks.

Article 13

(1) Everyone has the right to freedom of movement and residence within the borders of each state.

(2) Everyone has the right to leave any country, including his own, and to return to his country.

Article 14

(1) Everyone has the right to seek and to enjoy in other countries asylum from persecution.

(2) This right may not be invoked in the case of prosecutions genuinely arising from non-political crimes or from acts contrary to the purposes and principles of the United Nations.

Article 15

(1) Everyone has the right to a nationality.

(2) No one shall be arbitrarily deprived of his nationality nor denied the right to change his nationality.

Article 16

(1) Men and women of full age, without any limitation due to race, nationality or religion, have the right to marry and to found a family. They are entitled to equal rights as to marriage, during marriage and at its dissolution.

(2) Marriage shall be entered into only with the free and full consent of the intending spouses.

(3) The family is the natural and fundamental group unit of society and is entitled to protection by society and the State.

Article 17

(1) Everyone has the right to own property alone as well as in association with others.

(2) No one shall be arbitrarily deprived of his property.

Article 18

Everyone has the right to freedom of thought, conscience and religion; this right includes freedom to change his religion or belief, and freedom, either alone or in community with others and in public or private, to manifest his religion or belief in teaching, practice, worship and observance.

Article 19

Everyone has the right to freedom of opinion and expression; this right includes freedom to hold opinions without interference and to seek, receive and impart information and ideas through any media and regardless of frontiers.

Article 20

(1) Everyone has the right to freedom of peaceful assembly and association.

(2) No one may be compelled to belong to an association.

Article 21

(1) Everyone has the right to take part in the government of his country, directly or through freely chosen representatives.

(2) Everyone has the right of equal access to public service in his country.

(3) The will of the people shall be the basis of the authority of government; this will shall be expressed in periodic and genuine elections which shall be by universal and equal suffrage and shall be held by secret vote or by equivalent free voting procedures.

Article 22

Everyone, as a member of society, has the right to social security and is entitled to realization, through national effort and international co-operation and in accordance with the organization and resources of each State, of the economic, social and cultural rights indispensable for his dignity and the free development of his personality.

Article 23

(1) Everyone has the right to work, to free choice of employment, to just and favorable conditions of work and to protection against unemployment.

(2) Everyone, without any discrimination, has the right to equal pay for equal work.

(3) Everyone who works has the right to just and favorable remuneration ensuring for himself and his family an existence worthy of human dignity, and supplemented, if necessary, by other means of social protection.

(4) Everyone has the right to form and to join trade unions for the protection of his interests.

Article 24

Everyone has the right to rest and leisure, including reasonable limitation of working hours and periodic holidays with pay.

Article 25

(1) Everyone has the right to a standard of living adequate for the health and well-being of himself and of his family, including food,

clothing, housing and medical care and necessary social services, and the right to security in the event of unemployment, sickness, disability, widowhood, old age or other lack of livelihood in circumstances beyond his control.

(2) Motherhood and childhood are entitled to special care and assistance. All children, whether born in or out of wedlock, shall enjoy the same social protection.

Article 26

(1) Everyone has the right to education. Education shall be free, at least in the elementary and fundamental stages. Elementary education shall be compulsory. Technical and professional education shall be made generally available and higher education shall be equally accessible to all on the basis of merit.

(2) Education shall be directed to the full development of the human personality and to the strengthening of respect for human rights and fundamental freedoms. It shall promote understanding, tolerance and friendship among all nations, racial or religious groups, and shall further the activities of the United Nations for the maintenance of peace.

(3) Parents have a prior right to choose the kind of education that shall be given to their children.

Article 27

(1) Everyone has the right freely to participate in the cultural life of the community, to enjoy the arts and to share in scientific advancement and its benefits.

(2) Everyone has the right to the protection of the moral and material interests resulting from any scientific, literary or artistic production of which he is the author.

Article 28

Everyone is entitled to a social and international order in which the rights and freedoms set forth in this Declaration can be fully realized.

Article 29

(1) Everyone has duties to the community in which alone the free and full development of his personality is possible.

(2) In the exercise of his rights and freedoms, everyone shall be subject only to such limitations as are determined by law solely for the purpose of securing due recognition and respect for the rights and freedoms of others and of meeting the just requirements of morality, public order and the general welfare in a democratic society.

(3) These rights and freedoms may in no case be exercised contrary to the purposes and principles of the United Nations.

Article 30

Nothing in this Declaration may be interpreted as implying for any State, group or person any right to engage in any activity or to perform any act aimed at the destruction of any of the rights and freedoms set forth herein.

CPSIA information can be obtained at www.ICGtesting.com
Printed in the USA
BVOW031622141012

302910BV00002B/1/P